fr. Griffin, S.J.

What reviewers have said about LIVING IN HOPE:

"Hope is 'in' this theology season, and here Jesuit Father Boros gives this 'in' thing an up-dated Catholic definition, in terms of life and after-life, tangibles (e.g. suffering) and intangibles (e.g. soul). Boros is brief but surprisingly effective. His is the sort of meditative theology of which the church is in crying need, and with which precious few are preoccupied." *The Critic*

"These short chapters, which are more 'sentences' or 'meditations' on hope than a technical theological exposé, manage to achieve the depth and freshness that we have come to expect from the mind of this 'existential' theologian. Perhaps the appeal of the author's work lies in the fact that his approach to Christ bears the conviction of a lived experience." *The Sign*

"Boros situates hope as the basic structure of human existence and the essence of the Christian message. He reminds the Christian that living a life of hope means having a fundamental optimism, 'that there is still joy, happiness and hope in the world, that life is good and worth living.'" *The Catholic World*

"A book for meditative reading, LIVING IN HOPE is a must. It belongs in the same category with the other spiritual writings by the same author . . . The translation by W. J. O'Hara is as smooth as silk." *Catholic Messenger*

D0556100

Living in Hope

Living in Hope

Future Perspectives in Christian Thought

by LADISLAUS BOROS, S.J.

Translated by W. J. O'HARA

IMAGE BOOKS
A Division of Doubleday & Company, Inc.
Garden City, New York

Image Books edition 1973
by special arrangement with Herder and Herder
Image Books edition published February 1973

This is a translation of Aus der Hoffnung leben
(*Walter-Verlag, Olten and Freiburg im Breisgau, 1968*)

Nihil obstat: JOHN M. T. BARTON, S.T.D., L.S.S., Censor
Imprimatur: ✠ PATRICK CASEY, Vicar General
  Westminster: 31 July 1969

ISBN: 0-385-00133-9
© Walter-Verlag AG, Olten, 1968
English translation © Burns & Oates Ltd 1969

Contents

Preface

This book will attempt to define human life in terms of hope and to formulate the question of God in the light of man's expectations for the future. Christian inquiry must be directed to what is open, not yet final and settled, still to come. For hope is not just one item in Christian life; it is the absolutely indispensable condition for actually engaging in that life. The "God of hope" is the driving force of the Christian understanding of human existence. To be directed towards the future in hope is a feature of the whole Christian message, of the Church, of every Christian life and therefore of all reflection on its mystery. Hope is the goal and tendency of all Christian life, thought and prayer. Christianity itself might even be summed up as the faith in which God unreservedly ratifies men's hope, yet surpasses it so immeasurably that the boldest aspirations and most presumptuous dreams of the human heart appear fainthearted in comparison. In a Christian and hopeful spirit of this kind, these meditations will speak about the joyful element in our life and the promise it holds for the future.

Living in Hope

FACING THE FUTURE

Origin and Goal of Life

MAN is a being who faces the future. The process of anthropogenesis is not yet complete. Both biologically and mentally man is only at the beginning of his evolution. Natural scientists actually promise incalculable vistas of time for his development. Palaeontologists speak of 50 million years as the probable lifetime of a zoological species of average size. This alone shows what immense problems man has to contend with today if he is to come to terms with his future. It is splendid, but at the same time dangerous, to stand at the spear-point of evolution, to advance into a future whose dangers and promises we cannot even surmise. A new science is coming into existence, the science of the future. To develop it in a Christian spirit is one of the most important tasks of Christian thinkers at the present time.

The Christian has an absolute future in front of him, which quite simply is called heaven. Nowadays a Christian chiefly wants to hear something about heaven which he will find humanly conceivable. Unfortunately we cannot help noticing time and time again that the lamest and most colourless sections of our theological treatises are precisely those devoted to heaven. For my own part, if I have to prepare a sermon on heaven, about our own real future, I open a book by the Marxist Ernst Bloch, *Prinzip Hoffnung*. In it I find an astonishingly accurate analysis of what it is in us that aspires to an absolute future. This is surely a cause for shame for the Christian thinker. After all, it ought to be our most important and most Christian task to bear witness even as thinkers to the existence of heaven, of a heaven which we can not merely abstractly conceive, but which we experience daily and hourly in the depth of all we live and know. If nowadays we do speak honestly about heaven on the basis of our genuine human experiences, people pay attention.

Ernst Bloch's philosophy of hope, with its wealth of analyses, makes the Christian thinker realize how little and how bloodlessly we Christians speak of the kingdom of heaven which has already entered into our world. There is serious ground here for an examination of conscience. For we, of all people, bear the mark of the "principle of hope," in our very flesh so to speak. Yet it has become quite a fashion for us to talk largely about the lamentable state of mankind. Some people have even made something of a name for themselves in literature by it. But hope, fundamental optimism, the taste for happiness, are part of the very element which is vital for human life. If the Christian is to be God's witness, and even a witness to God's greatness, there is perhaps one thing above all others which he must do today, and that is to prove to his fellow men that there is still joy, happiness and hope in the world, that life is good and worth living.

Where does life, and reality in general, come from? From God. My origin is in God. What does that mean? I, with all that makes me what I am, am shaped according to God's pattern. I live as one of God's thoughts. The very fact of being created means that we bear God's life in us, and in virtue of our actual constitution are designed for an eternal glorification. Life was fashioned by God with heaven in view. Consequently man must be understood in the light of his perfect fulfilment, heaven. What happens before that fulfilment is merely man's coming to birth. The world only attains existence when man enters heaven. We are not yet alive in the real and fullest sense of the word. Our life is still in process of coming to be, with heaven as its goal. Life pure and simple is not yet there; its real form is still coming towards us. What man really is still lies ahead.

One of the most remarkable facts about the development of modern thought is that man is becoming more and more aware of his solidarity with the world. He no longer regards this world as a static reality, however, but rather as the unity of an evolutionary process. This comprises the formation of an ordered universe with its milky ways, solar systems and planets, the production of primitive and then of progressively more complex forms of life, a groping advance towards even higher forms of consciousness. Man is the product of this evolution, the flowering of the world. The interiority of the world, so to speak, is concentrated in man. The universe develops from its original condition in the direction of life. Life evolves towards man by transforming itself into spirit. Spirit takes possession of itself by coming to know God and dedicating itself to him in love. The union of man with God draws the cosmos into eternal fulfilment.

This fulfilment is a universe which has finally become transparent to God. The cosmos therefore, according to this account, is a single evolutionary proc-

ess. God is constantly creating the world by endowing
it with the forces necessary for it to raise itself towards
him in a development extending over thousands of
millions of years. The history of the creation of the
world runs as follows. In God's eternally one act of
creation, which is both beginning and fulfilment in
one, a space was inserted as it were for the self-
development of the creation, and in this, by the power
of God, the cosmos by an evolutionary process extending over thousands of millions of years culminates in
man, through whom it then enters into an absolute
future, that is, heaven.

The Letter to the Colossians says of Christ, "In him
all things were created, in heaven and on earth . . .
all things were created through him and for him"
(1:16). Christ is therefore the absolute outcome and
goal. The movement of cosmic evolution is directed
towards Christ. It follows that Christ is still in process
of becoming. One of the profoundest insights of
Christian doctrine is indicated here. Christ did indeed
come to us for a moment, as it were, but immediately
disappeared into the inscrutable future, which may
extend for millions of years. Christ continues until the
end of time in process of coming to be. Consequently
the Christian is a human being whose life is developing into something radically different, an unsurpassable future. If there is a world, and human beings
with longings and aspirations, then heaven must exist,
for man can only exist by understanding himself as
hope and as unsurpassable hope at that.

The Christian conception of history is therefore a
message of joy. The fate of the world is already decided. No quest ends in the void. Where there is still
life, a flame of love however small, the final creation,
heaven, is already perceptible. In a world of that kind

there is no reason for despair and faintheartedness. The souls our God wants to see are joyful, fresh, invigorated, carefree, not broken and wilted. This is fundamentally the frame of mind in which a Christian should think about the fact that he is created, and view his future. He ought to banish gloom and sombre thoughts from his soul. They are not good for anything. They miss the real point. A Christian life ought to express, and in fact be based on, the attitude that life is still developing in us, that the universe is also comprised in the redemption and will come to its completion in Christ, that God has prepared an eternal joy for us.

Perhaps one final consideration would not be out of place here. The goal, the ultimate fulfilment, is to share in God. But no created being can receive in its fullness and exhaust God's limitless plenitude. Our finite entity can never totally coincide with God's reality. Consequently each fulfilment is also the beginning of even greater fulfilment. Heaven must be understood as essentially an infinite dynamism. Our very fulfilment itself will extend our scope, make us more than we are so that we can then be filled even more by the illimitable. We are seeking God eternally. A Father of the Church, Augustine, aptly says that we seek God in order to find him, during our earthly life. We seek God after we have found him, in eternal happiness, in heaven. So that we may seek and find him, he is hidden. So that we may seek him after we have found him, he is immeasurable. Our eternity will be a continual advance further into God.

Everything static is drawn in heaven into a limitless dynamism extending without end. Beatitude is eternal transformation. There is nothing fixed and rigid in heaven, which is a condition of unending and unbroken vitality.

When this comes about, and every longing has at last found fulfilment, the sublime adventure of creation will have reached its end. And the real creation will begin, with the fulfilment of heart's desire. "Then I saw a new heaven and a new earth . . . God . . . will wipe away every tear from their eyes and death shall be no more, neither shall there be mourning nor crying nor pain any more . . ." (Rev. 21:1, 4). To be a Christian means to live this hope and bear witness by it, in every situation in life, even the most difficult.

Have We a Soul?

IT is perhaps remarkable that a priest of all people should ask this question, or even risk asking it. But we are living in strange times. Our faith itself compels us to think out every kind of question afresh, right from the very foundations. The present problem, however, should, I think, be phrased differently and run, "What does it mean for me to have an 'exterior' and an 'interior,' 'a without and a within'?"—"How do I experience the human situation in the world?"—"How does it affect me with its commonplace, cramping character but at the same time with its hope and impulse towards what is unknown and has not yet been experienced?"

Everyday experience shows that we have in us something that continually bursts our cramping limits, our lassitude and narrow lives—a hope, a drive towards something higher, an expectation. Yet at the same time it is our lot to be confined in a situation of narrow limits. We have something in us which we can never realize, express, find words for. Philosophy has attempted to explain this tension of our existence between openness to the infinite and confinement within the narrow limits of the immediate foreground. Philosophy spoke of man as consisting of soul and body. This was meant to explain the profound disharmony in our experience. It was an attempt to grasp the mystery of man in concepts. The real question ought therefore to run, "What lies behind the fact that I am simultaneously aware of myself as without limits and as limited?"

If we are to think this question out afresh, we must go back to the simplest facts of our human existence which are accessible and comprehensible to everyone. Let us imagine, by way of experiment, a human being who has lived out his human life from birth to death in full accordance with its inherent dynamism. What has taken place in such a life? A double line can be traced through it.

In the first place, a human life involves a sort of explosive "expansion." The expression here does not refer only to the "body" but to the whole human being inasmuch as his life is turned outwards. But what does this "outwards" mean? In the first place it is the growth of the biological powers, self-development and maturation of the organism, specialization of the various faculties, growth in knowledge, awakening to friendship, widening of the horizons, mastery of the world and of self, love. A human life "grows into" the world. But as a man throws himself into his work in the world, into externals, the world begins to wear away his powers. Youthful *élan* slackens, vital energies flow less abundantly. The human being sees with terrifying clarity that despite occasional successes and despite his creative activity in the world, he has not really achieved what he had dreamt and hoped. He has failed in what really matters, in his work and influence, in honesty, friendship, love. He has not been equal to the demands made on him. And so it goes on, inexorably. He becomes lonely, and faces his own failure in solitude. He becomes a burden to others, and this is perhaps the hardest thing to bear. In the end he collapses, and with him everything that he has built up in the world with so much toil, love, effort and unselfishness. The "outer man" has worn himself out. But is that all human life is? Certainly not.

Precisely by coming up against one's own limits, in the experience of outward collapse, something important happens, if a human life is honestly lived out to its end—the inner man comes to maturity. In the crises and difficulties of all kinds, as the outer man becomes worn out, something is built up to which the term "person" may be applied. In a genuinely human life the energies of the outer man are not simply squandered to no purpose, but are transformed into an interiority. A living centre forms within a human being who keeps trying to make a fresh start despite failure and breakdown, who realizes the dangers and stands his ground, profiting by every situation, even the most difficult, to grow inwardly. In this way, slowly and silently the mature human being takes shape. Something hidden and sacred emerges, a personal existence, conscious of its narrow confines yet living its way into infinity, capable of silence amid the din of things and events because inwardly recollected. Interiority as authentic as this is achieved in most cases only at the end of a sorely tried life. A very characteristic strength pervades it, that of gentleness and unobtrusive goodwill.

By dint of overcoming the crises of the outer man, and only thereby, genuine interiority is achieved. And as a consequence the world becomes more transparent. A new dimension of cosmic reality develops. Out of the joys and afflictions of the momentous days of a lifetime, the inner self slowly crystallizes. It is a self precisely because it has become selfless. The outer has become an inner life. Man becomes the centre of reality.

The answer to our original question ought therefore to be that man has a soul, but at the same time has to make a soul for himself. He has the task of becoming a man of interior life. It is his mission to catch a glimpse, through things, of something which it is quite impossible to assemble out of mere particular items of knowledge, namely the reason of reasons, the reality of all that exists, what transcends all the branches of knowledge. He is charged with maintaining a longing within himself. He has to live his friendship and his love in such a way that vistas of infinity open out through them. The more the vital powers fade, the more there develops, or should develop, out of all that a man has experienced, achieved, endured and won by love, something which irradiates the world with kindness, understanding, goodwill, justice and mercy.

Man's interiority, whch is what we are accustomed to designate by the word "soul," is not simply present in the world as a datum. Even in an embryo something is present, of course, which impels its subsequent higher development. Consequently we have to safeguard and protect it. What is merely present in this way, however, has to be brought to its full reality through freedom. That is the task we face because we are human. Everyone must have this possibility at some point. When and how does this occur? At some point means, at least in death. Every human being must have the chance of bringing the external (which we call the body) into the interior realm, of opening himself to the Absolute.

One of the greatest Christian thinkers, Thomas Aquinas, though still hampered by the soul-body schema, puts forward a suggestion of this kind. According to him, man does not consist of two "things" but has a single nature in which matter and spirit form a single substance; the two constitute a third, which is identical with neither of them separately. The human body is the expression of the soul while, conversely, the human soul is the highest realization of matter. Aquinas repeatedly emphasizes that the human soul enters into matter necessarily, in virtue of its very nature. Without its body there is no human soul. The two are principles of human reality united in a substantial union. Man is a single reality, not a combination of two substances. The body is essentially actuated by the soul. The soul's relation to the body belongs to its very essence. Corporeality is the unfolding of what *in radice* is contained in the soul. Conversely the soul is what the "tendency" of matter necessarily and essentially aspires to. This philosophical intuition is probably one of the most important ideas put forward in the history of thought. Furthermore, it shows that a man who thinks in terms of ultimate principles, even if he is confined by firmly organized formulas and concepts, can break out of these from within and anticipate ideas which mankind will only fully comprehend centuries later. It is already possible to see what far-ranging conclusions can be drawn from these considerations for our next theme—death. But it is too early to draw these inferences at this point.

In essentials, however, the answer is already implicit here. What we can say on the basis of our Christian and secular consciousness, independently of any particular conceptual schema, is that man is the being produced by the effort of a cosmic evolution during thousands of millions of years. In him the forces of the cosmos striving for interiorization converge. In him matter can move forward to become conscious of an Absolute, and thus attain permanence for ever. Man is limitless tension towards the infinite, but at the same time a fragile and self-consuming entity, separate from the world and at the same time an intrinsic part of it. Is this the reality which until now has been called soul and body? If so, soul and body exist. I think, however, that at long last we should start to think more in terms of wholes. We are bound up with the universe. We are its culmination. In us it enters into direct contact with God. In us the cosmos knows God, loves him or, we must not forget, hates him. This is the strange reality in us which thinkers for thousands of years have called "the soul." It is both hope and threat.

Unfortunately our reflections became too philosophical. We have only been concerned to show that it is possible to think about man in different terms from those we have been used to so far. The important point, however we phrase it, is to hold firm to one thing, namely, that being human involves an openness without limits, and at the same time a threatening narrowness and constriction. The words and expressions we use to denote this, matter little. What does matter is for us to bring about in our lives the very movement of the universe, closer and closer to God. This is only possible, however, unfortunately or fortunately as we choose to regard it, by our dying into God and thus saving the world which produced us, and bringing it into the eternal glory of the resurrection.

Death as Decision

In death comes the possibility of man's first fully personal action. Consequently death is the point of full consciousness, freedom and decision regarding one's eternal lot. This rather academic statement is meant to convey the following idea. It is only at the moment of death that man can set aside the strangeness of his own existence. Only in death does he become ontologically strong enough and sufficiently concentrated in mind to meet Christ totally with all the elements of his being and to make a final decision about him. According to this view, therefore, in the moment of death we should have another chance of decision. More precisely, only in death does the first possibility occur of making a total, fully personal choice. According to this hypothesis, therefore, every human being in death has the possibility of deciding about Christ, in full possession of his powers, with full lucidity and total freedom.

"In death." Much depends on understanding this expression correctly. It is not a matter of the situation before death. It is not really possible to suppose that someone will posit the first full personal act of his life in the state of bodily pain and mental dullness of the death agony. Nor, on the other hand, is it a question of the state after death.

After death our eternal lot is fixed for ever. In death we have reached finality in such a way that nothing can alter it any more. It is therefore a question of the actual moment of death itself.

When the soul, that interior reality of which we spoke in our last meditation, leaves the body, it suddenly awakens to its own pure spirituality, and is wholly filled with light and clarity. It understands at once all that a created spirit can know and understand. It sees its entire life as a single whole. It perceives within it God's call and guidance. It is also confronted with the whole cosmos illumined in its totality by the risen Lord as the ultimate mystery of the universe. For, as the Letter to the Ephesians testifies, the Lord by his resurrection and ascension fills all things. In death, then, man is free, with full knowledge, capable of making a final decision. This decision involves the highest and clearest encounter with Christ of his life. It is impossible for him now to pass Christ by. He must choose. And what is thus decided, in death, remains for ever, because a man puts his whole self into this commitment and makes up his mind once and for all. And as he has decided, so he lives for ever. His eternity will be simply the actual unfolding of what occurs at that moment.

Until death, a man is not yet in full possession of himself. He lives in continual longing anticipation of what he will be, he can never catch up with himself at any point. He lives in inner dissension and is therefore incapable of achieving what he is called to by what he most truly is. His life cannot come to fruition during life. His own essential being always lies ahead of him. He cannot yet be said to *be* in the proper sense

of the term; he is merely a continual process of becoming. Consequently man also remains a stranger in
the world, a stranger in regard to things, to persons
and to events. Above all, he is and remains a stranger
to himself. He throws himself into the future in order
to exist. Consequently he merely skims the passing moment as it were; he merely touches his own life at a
tangent, he does not really live it. He cannot give his
life its full scope or be what he essentially is in an un-
divided present. Only at the moment when he no
longer goes on any further into the same fragmented
future can he accomplish what he is. Then the pent-
up waters of his life burst forth and at last he *is*. He no
longer lives like a rushing mountain torrent but like a
calm mountain lake, clear and deep, mirroring the
whole splendour of the world. Such a moment can
only come in death, for only then is there no further
advance in the same direction, into the empty void of
time. In death a life dawns which consists of a cease-
less present. Only in death does man attain the total
unity of what he is. He escapes from the limits which
hem in his life on all sides, and enters into a profound
dimension of the world, the very heart of the universe.

As a symbolic expression for what happens at death,
the image of birth at once suggests itself. At birth the
child is forcibly expelled from the limits of its mother's
womb and has to leave what was protective, familiar
and dear. It is exposed, and threatened with total de-
struction. At the same time a vast new world opens
out before it, a new relation to the world of light, colours, meanings, human company and love. Something similar happens to man in death. He is taken by
force from the narrow bounds of his previous connection with the world. At the same time he attains a
new and essential relation to the world, one which

links him with the whole breadth of cosmic reality. Man therefore really perishes, in the sense of being reduced to nothing by the forcible deprivation of his corporeal reality. At the same time he is plunged to the very roots of the world and so acquires a cosmic relation to reality, a pancosmic presence. This ground of the world into which man descends in death is of its nature open to Christ, transparent to the radical ground of all that exists. Man in death is also confronted with all that he had always most deeply desired, what he had guessed at in all he knew, striven for without realizing it in whatever he willed, embraced, had he but known it, in all his love. In all this he is confronted with the "Lord of the world." This is the metaphysical point where he will make his final decision. Christ stands there in front of man, in death; clearly seen, luminously perceived, summoning him to himself with the gesture of redeeming love. Man has only to decide. Judgment depends on him. Christ will always be there with the same loving summons and readiness to give. If a man decides against Christ, it makes no difference at all to Christ's love. But that love will sear him eternally because he rejects it. If he decides for Christ, Christ's self-same love will be an everlasting light for him and his final fulfilment in happiness without bounds.

God is not petty. He is magnanimous. No one is damned merely by chance, because he was suddenly called to eternity by an accident, or because he had never properly come to know God in his lifetime, or because he was born into a family where he never knew what love is and so could never understand what God himself is, or because he perhaps turned against a God in whom he saw nothing but a God of the law, a dreadful tyrant, or because he was hated, rejected, misjudged and wounded to the heart by human beings and so rebelled against everything, including God. Conversely, however, no one attains eternal salvation merely because he had pious parents, or because his bourgeois prejudices kept him from doing the evil he would so much have liked to do, or because he, unlike thousands of millions of human beings, had the good fortune to grow up in a part of the world where one can still occasionally hear something about Christ, or because it so happened he had a pleasant disposition and so knew what it was to be loved and did not find it difficult to believe that God too loved him.

No one is damned unless he has decided against God with his whole being, in full clarity and reflection. But neither is he divinized unless he has embraced God most closely with every fibre of his soul. It does not matter where he was born, when he died, what kind of temperament he inherited. Every human being has the chance to decide in full clarity for or against Christ. In this perspective, which we put forward here as a new basis for reflection, it is easier to understand that the judgment and God's universal will to save are terms between which there is a profound harmony. Every human being has the possibility at least once of meeting the risen Christ, of coming to know him personally. Every single human being has this chance. Even the pagans, those millions who have not yet heard anything of Christ, even the paganized Christians to whom we have perhaps preached a tedious, unreal God whom they could never really appreciate and learn to love, even those human beings who from the religious and moral point of view have remained little children, although their faculties in other respects have developed quite normally and who can cope quite successfully with the complicated structure of modern life, even those people who hate God because they regard him, for example, as an instrument of capitalist exploitation and have never known him in his true nature, even the feeble-minded and mentally defective who have never been able to understand anything properly, even the stillborn children and babies who die without baptism, and finally we ourselves, who are too weak to do good and whose hearts remain so cold and empty. All have the opportunity of attaining salvation in a full personal meeting with Christ.

The objection is often made to our conception of human death as final decision that if we have a final opportunity for decision in death, why should we be in a hurry to begin now to live a Christian life? Is this an objection? Not at all. For what and who can assure me that I will take the right decision? The outcome of that final decision will depend on me. There is no other criterion of the honesty of my wish for conversion then except conversion here and now. What I should like to be in the future I must begin in the present. I must practise by the many small decisions of my life for the great final decision in death. I must be converted and at once, if I honestly wish to be converted at death. Any postponement is a living lie. I cannot simply live my life away heedlessly, leaving everything to the final decision. Who can guarantee that at the end I shall change the bent of a lifetime? The idea of a final chance to decide at death does not lessen in the slightest our vigilance regarding salvation.

Our hypothesis provides a simple and humane solution to various theological problems. Here I shall refer only to the question of purgatory. From the point of view of the hypothesis we are proposing, our death, the moment of our final decision for Christ, is at the same time our purgatory. The place of purification is not some kind of torture-chamber or cosmic concentration camp, in which wretched lamenting and sighing creatures are punished by God. God's thoughts cannot be so grotesque and unworthy. Purgatory is rather the meeting with Christ, having to sustain the fire of his loving gaze which is our ultimate purification. Full of love and rich in grace, Christ looks at the human being approaching him. But that gaze burns into the innermost, most secret essence of human reality. To meet God in the flame of Christ's gaze is indeed the highest fulfilment of our capacity for love, but at the same time it means the most terrible suffering in our very essence. In this perspective, purgatory would mean passing through the flame of Christ's love, a momentary event in the meeting with Christ in death. At this meeting, love for God breaks out from the depths of human reality, and as it does so it must as it were pierce the strata and deposits of our own self-seeking. The whole of this human reality must appear before the Christ who is approaching it with his love. The harder and more stubborn these layers of egotism, the more painful the eruption of the love of God, and the more purifying the meeting with Christ. Individual human beings would therefore each personally undergo at the moment of death a process of purification which would differ in intensity for each. Thus, instead of a difference in the time spent in purgatory, there would be a difference in the degree of intensity of the purification.

Our hypothesis may also perhaps suggest a way to a less superficial idea of heaven. By living through the terror of meeting God in this loving approach to

Christ, the human being has left behind everything about God which imperils our finite being. The danger is over; the human being can enter into the knowledge and love of Christ, which of course is what heaven is. Heaven would thus be the unfolding into a state of being of the choice of Christ made in death, while purgatory would mean what makes it possible to enjoy Christ's company with serene happiness for ever.

When Does the Resurrection Take Place?

WHAT fate awaits the world? We shall start with the essential, Christ's resurrection. Christ is risen. He has, our faith tells us, overcome all the limitations of human existence. What man really is was made visible in him. Consequently, if we wish to speak about the future as Christians, our reflection must start with a consideration of the risen Christ. In him we see the mode of being in which human reality finds its perfect fulfilment. For our purposes we should like to draw a distinction between two aspects of the resurrection; they are nevertheless merely two sides of one and the same reality.

The first of these aspects is the descent into hell. Before the death of the redeemer there was no heaven. The Letter to the Hebrews says, "The way into the sanctuary was not yet open." Christ's death broke down the wall of the world. The world once again became God's place, the *"milieu divin."* Christ's reality pervaded the whole universe. Consequently the light first shone forth for those who until then had had to live imprisoned in the world. As we have already indicated, man in death emerges from his spatio-temporal limitation, extends through the universe, becomes pancosmic. He enters that essential domain of the universe from which all nature springs, the "heart of the universe." It was into this essential sphere of cosmic reality that the men of pre-Christian times died. With every human being who entered by death into this ground of the world, the world's longing increased, until it became a single appeal for deliverance and, as the Letter to the Romans says, the creation lay "groaning in travail." When Christ in his death entered into the whole of cosmic reality, all men of pre-Christian times knew him in a single moment. Everything became light, the light of knowledge and freedom. Thousands of millions of men in a single moment were confronted with the decisive choice of their lives. Then followed the eruption of the world to God. It is not surprising that the earth shook. In order to be able to redeem all men Christ himself "had to" die, enter into the ground of the world, so as to become present to all those who had died into the world. At this moment a movement extending over thousands of millions of years reached its goal. The universe is no longer the same as it was before. From now on Christ himself lives in all that is deep, essential and in the background. From now on, every death, every burial in the earth is an entry into Christ. The world has become holy. That is the genuine but frequently misunderstood sense of the article of faith: "He descended into hell, into the lower world" (the expression does not really mean "hell" in the proper sense of the word, but the innermost centre or heart of the world). Christ thus became the centre of the world and the innermost focus of all the impulses of the human heart.

The second dimension is the resurrection. Here the incomprehensible took place. An attentive reading of the accounts of the appearances of the risen Christ produces at first a confusing impression. The limitations of space and time no longer exist for Christ. He appears abruptly, suddenly walks with the disciples, disappears, comes into closed rooms. A new mode of being has appeared. The apostle says that Christ is "spirit." Here the expression does not mean a distinction from the body. It means taken up into a life which knows no bounds. Christ took his earthly life with him, transformed it into a new reality which includes the universe. His resurrection was not simply a return to his previous life, as in the case of the raising of Lazarus, for example, who was brought back into the limits of our human existence. The first sign for the apostles was the empty tomb. Fundamentally this means that Christ took his earthly body with him. He did not abandon his poor tortured human body. His human face that was buffeted remains to all eternity the face of God. That is the ultimate and deepest thing that can be said about our human life. Human reality has risen above the highest sphere of the universe and entered into the life of the blessed Trinity. The universe, which in a history extending over thousands of millions of years had converged on man, has returned to him from whose bosom it sprang unimaginable ages before. The risen Christ is the first-fruits, the beginning, the ultimate ground of the new life. With him the world set off for the definitive future. This brings us to the prime theme of our reflections.

Man will rise from the dead. What is a risen human being? We will preface this question with another preliminary one which may appear merely incidental but which will bring us close to the essential definition of man's resurrection. *When* does the resurrection from the dead take place? The ideas we are about to outline may perhaps appear hazardous, but we should like to put them forward as a basis for reflection.

On the one hand we usually think of the death of a human being as the separation of soul and body. In view of our previous considerations, however, is such a separation possible at all? We have noted that the soul by its very essence stands in relationship to matter. The soul cannot exist without the body. Man is one entity. It would be incongruous to say there was a soul without a body. Consequently the resurrection must take place straightway at the moment of death. There is no soul separated from the body, there is only the one single human being. This is the first point which must be taken into account.

On the other hand, revelation repeatedly emphasizes that man's resurrection from the dead is an eschatological event. It coincides with Christ's second coming at the Last Day. Consequently man's resurrection can only be conceived as taking place at the end of time. We are clearly faced by an *aporia,* a blind-alley of thought.

Karl Rahner has suggested the following solution. In death the human soul does not become "noncorporeal" but enters into a pancosmic relationship, and is present everywhere in the universe. He takes the view that at the moment of leaving the body, the human soul enters into a new relation to matter and becomes omnipresent in the material reality of the universe. I appreciate Karl Rahner's profound insight here and accept it, but I wonder why we need stop at this half-way solution. Why should the resurrection not take place at the same time as death? The more radical solution would be to say that the resurrection takes place immediately at death, but that it is an eschatological event nevertheless. This is only an apparent contradiction. The risen human being needs the transformed and transfigured universe as his dwelling place. The transformation at the end of time would therefore involve the final completion of the resurrection that had already occurred at death. Consequently it would be meaningful to say both that the resurrection takes place immediately at death and that the resurrection is an eschatological event at the end of time. This would mean that the human soul is never without a body; immortality and resurrection are in fact one and the same.

Now we can raise the central question. What is the risen human being? From revelation we merely know that the risen human being will be the perfect expression of the world united to God for ever. From this point of view it is at least possible to say what the risen human being will not be.

He will not suffer any pain. The resurrection in the first place implies freedom from suffering, that is, a condition which we long for with every fibre of our being. Revelation insists on this. The elect are consoled to the uttermost. In the Bible, however, freedom from suffering is merely the obverse of an infinite gift bestowed on man. God will totally penetrate man's being and consequently human existence will blossom out into its purest essence, and with it, the universe. This produces an ardent existence, which grows further and further into God, and is raised above all the hazards of its earthly vulnerability.

Man will no longer be a stranger to God. He will become the expression of the experience of immediate contact with God. We shall "hear," "taste" and "touch" God. God will be wholly present in human life. What does that mean? Since God is present everywhere, it means that in some sense man also will be "boundless."

This leads us to the third characteristic of the risen human being.

Man will know no more narrow limits. Everything spiritual will overflow into the senses and the latter into the former. Sight will become direct knowledge, touch will be recognition, and hearing will be understanding. The limits of space will disappear. Man will at once exist wherever his love, desire and happiness attract him. Human life in the state of resurrection will therefore be wholly "spirit," but that spirituality will simultaneously include that sweetness and joyous quality which derives from the earthly character of our senses. Can any of us honestly say that we should really wish eternally to be deprived of what the sight of a field of flowers, the embrace of a beloved person and the sound of a beautiful voice mean to us? The message of the resurrection is the most human of all that Christianity has announced to mankind.

Man is the perfection and "sum" of the universe which has produced him in a process stretching over thousands of millions of years. Man drawing his life entirely from God becomes the centre of the universe, the abode of the Absolute, the vessel of the holy. The world was created for this state to come about. Man only appears in his genuine reality at the resurrection. This is the central event of the making of the world, of cosmogenesis. The world is already redeemed. We human beings, however—it is the privilege of our freedom—have freely to carry up our reality into its final fulfilment. We can become "eternal" only by our free decision. By deciding in favour of Christ, and thus entering into a loving unity of existence with him, we attain unity in our own being, the glory of eternal growth into God. Then and only then we really become human beings. The end is the real beginning.

CHRISTIAN HOPE

Thinking in Hope

IN prayerful meditation, a human being concentrates his attention on the central meaning of his life, puts aside the everyday round with its dispersion, superficiality and disquiet, and allows the fundamental experiences of life, loneliness, hope, dread, joy, happiness, desire for love and friendship, to emerge. To go deeper into oneself is an experience that affects the whole personality. It is not concerned to sketch hasty theories about these fundamental realities, but simply confronts them. It evokes once again from the depths of the soul the fundamental experiences of human existence which have been buried under the bustle of everyday life, and struggles free to a genuine relation to reality. Beyond all systems, received opinions and formulas, it catches a fresh glimpse of the meaning of life.

It is with this kind of attitude of direct concern with mystery, in prayful consideration, that we should like to bring to mind the ultimate divine and human ground of our hope. Christian life is a fruit of hope. It is essentially prospective, forward-looking, a departure into the unknown, an exodus. Christ has gone before us into the mystery of an absolute future. To wait in hope is the vital element, the fundamental personal attitude to life in which alone the Christian can glimpse the real content of his faith.

The essential message of the new covenant is the announcement that in Christ a completely new dimension of reality has opened out, heaven. This grows to maturity in the children of God, in the brothers and sisters of Jesus Christ. Since then, man can no longer be understood in terms of the mere fact of his presence on the earth. His life is purposefully directed towards heaven, towards a condition which is near at hand yet still to come. What happens in the meantime, all the seeking and groping which constitutes the greater part of the history of mankind and of each one of us, is merely birth. The world only begins to exist when man enters heaven. In the strictest sense of the word, therefore, we are not yet living. We do not yet see, hear and comprehend the essential. Life is not yet there. It is approaching us, in the form of hope. To reflect on the concrete presuppositions of a theology of hope involves nothing less than tracing the dynamism inherent in all Christian thought. In this first meditation on hope we shall do no more than mention unsystematically a few conditions of Christian thinking in hope.

First there is the ability to question. For man to be able to go beyond the narrow limits of mere subsistence, he must repeatedly try to experience afresh how fragmented his personal life is and how fragile his thought. He must realize by experience that no amount of sagacity, calculation or appraisal can provide any information about the meaning which mysteriously pervades the universe. What is really significant is the incalculable, remote and unattainable. When he looks for an answer, man raises himself above the provisional, begins to live a personal life in hope, faces the incalculable. An answer is always a personal event. Furthermore, it involves uncertainty and danger. The endeavour to go to meet the God of hope by the actual exercise of personal thought is a process in which man perpetually finds himself in what is new, surprising, unique and extreme. He gazes into the *terra incognita* of reality. The human answer is not a possession, but a process and a journey.

An essential feature of Christian meditation on mystery is apparent here. Contemplative insight cannot be strung together out of individual experiences, nor can it be taught or communicated at all; it is a most fundamental endowment of the soul. It is not concerned with partial connections but with the totality and uniqueness of the promise vouched for by hope. It proves nothing, but opens itself to what cannot be known. By it, man experiences something intrinsically complete even in the most insignificant things and happenings in the world. And so before the prayerful gaze there unfolds that divine realm which is familiar to all who lead an interior life. It is a realm of danger and risk, of ever new beginnings and change, of an open mind and of depth, the realm of hope. It is the realm of holy insecurity. What is creative is always at the very edge of reality. Anyone who does not surrender his very soul can neither attain his own soul nor be given over to God. Such meditation and contemplation in hope is perhaps our most Christian duty at the present time. In particular, in our thought and contemplation we must create unity out of superficial dualities; see meaningful unity in the world; descend again and again and more and more deeply into the abyss of transforming power in things, which is called God.

The prayerful questioning of Christian meditation constantly takes the form of sentences with two of the most fateful words in human language, "why?" and "I" (with their numerous derivatives). "Why was my existence forced upon me? Why was I not consulted? Why in the end am I deprived of everything that I have built up during life, worked to achieve, come to love? Why does God permit so much suffering? Why does he not help us just when we need him most? Why must we watch people we love tossed on a sea of sorrow and despair, dread and horror—perhaps endlessly? Does such a life hold any promise? What kind of a God are we at the mercy of, in such humiliation?"

And so the questions follow one another, work in us, obscure our original certainty. They can become so pressing that our whole faith is shaken and we have the feeling we are fools to go on believing. But the bitter experience of such perplexed, doubting inquiry and questioning is the primary condition for reflection on mystery, of thought in hope. The need to question is a mark of election, at once grace and task. It imposes itself on us, as though it were part of the human lot, an incomprehensible yet familiar power. It rises from the depths of the subconscious. It is like love, an inner necessity, an impulse which we freely accept; once we have become conscious of it, it holds us tenaciously in its power. It is therefore inherent in human existence to realize that as regards essentials, even those susceptible of an answer, there is nothing settled once and for all; doubt is therefore a possibility. The Christian thinker must risk his own soul for each answer. And even then he does not know whether his answer is the correct one. His mute prayer always continues to be, "Lord, I believe, help my unbelief."

This already brings us to another fundamental presupposition of thinking in hope, namely the ability to fall silent. Revelation, the object of Christian meditation, is not a perfectly complete system; it happens, it is a history. It is the history of man with God and, as becomes clear in Christ, of God with man. We have also to consider that God has only revealed sufficient for us to be able to risk the next step towards him in hope, into the darkness, trusting that his light will continue to shine for us. God has revealed to us everything that helps us to get to heaven, no more and no less. To many questions revelation gives no answer at all. God simply shows us uttermost love, even to the death on the cross. This self-sacrificing love is the ultimate manifestation of God; and the revelation of what God has not yet revealed to us and perhaps never will. Unfortunately the questions which revelation does not answer are precisely the ones which often distress us most bitterly. The question of suffering, for example, which the Bible never deals with theoretically. The Book of Job is the supreme expression of man's muteness in the face of suffering.

Attempts are often made to give a rational justification of suffering. On the lines, for example, that suffering is just as important for life as shadow and darkness are to show up the light more prominently. If we had nothing but this deplorable, threadbare and superficial answer to human suffering, we should have good reason to rebel. Anyone who has even once seen a child in pain, a child in the agony of death, a child crying to us for help which we cannot give, will know once and for all that all the beauty of the world, all the joy and radiance of the creation cannot justify the suffering of a single child. But we Christians cannot pay any heed to people who have an explanation for everything and who give a glib answer precisely when they have none. We ought rather honestly to admit that we do not understand God; that we do not understand why God has created pain, so much and such meaningless pain; why Christ's eyes at the end, on the cross, were so filled with grief and tears that he could not even recognize God. God gives no answer to human suffering. He took it upon himself. He allowed the sea of pain around him to surge into the very depth of his incarnate life.

Matthew tells us that "he began to be sorrowful and troubled" (26:37). Mark says, even more forcefully, "he began to be greatly distressed and troubled" (14:33), while Luke says that Christ was "in an agony" (22:43). In the Garden of Olives Christ's whole bodily and mental existence contracted into such a vital appeal that "his sweat became like drops of blood falling down upon the ground" (Luke 22:44). In face of this action of God, all questioning falls silent, although it presents no justification of suffering. Ability to fall silent in this way constitutes one of the creative features of meditation in hope. The finest and truly helpful words often spring from a silence permeated with suffering. God speaks to us through human beings who have suffered and passed through the loneliness of human distress. Their suffering has become their vocation and mission; they feel an inner bond with all who suffer. God has made them experience human distress so that one day they can sit down by a stranger, on the grey plank-bed of his private prison, and say, "Take hope, you are not alone." Such people have earned the right to bear the sufferings of others.

Here we recognize a third condition for thinking in

hope, fraternity. The human being who questions and falls silent in his questioning is acutely aware of the futility of superficial systems. He realizes the hopelessness of human endeavours to construct something permanent and valid. Consequently he does not judge, does not condemn, no longer divides the world into categories of enemies and friends, of likes and dislikes. He knows by personal experience, not merely by intellectual deduction from abstract proofs, that Christ suffered and died for all men and willed to give hope to all, that all men are subject to Christ's gentle rule, belong to him, are his inalienable possession.

The Christian who hopes is profoundly disturbed by the existential venture implied in the words of Christ which describe the conditions for inheriting the kingdom, the direct contact with God for which he hopes. Christ does not mention God himself at all, only the brother to whom we gave food, drink, shelter, clothes, whom we visited in sickness or in prison. This idea is given extremely radical form in John, who says that God loved us in order that we might love one another. As though Christ were not at all concerned for us explicitly to know and love him. Love of our neighbour is sufficient. As concrete expression of his love for God, man has nothing but his neighbour, here on earth and above in eternity. By his very nature he is dependent on brotherly love as a condition which makes his faith possible. There is no other way for him and no other way for his Christian thought. Finite love, dedication to the creature, with no further aim beyond actual attachment to a Thou who is in affliction yet nevertheless a source of happiness, is in itself love of God, hope, faith and prayer. Everyone who loves honestly and faithfully, directly and consciously experiences what God's reality is, even if he

has never yet heard of God. God has so sanctified finite, created love that in the end nothing remains out
of all human life, and even out of Christian life, faith,
hope, sacraments, prayer and Church, except such finite, created love.

Who is a Christian? All who are baptized, baptized
into the mind of Christ. Human beings who have received baptism, either in its full sacramental form
(baptism of water) or by the total sacrifice of their
life (baptism of blood) or implicitly by a profound
desire not yet conceptually formulated and which may
be impossible to formulate here and now (baptism of
desire). The slightest heartfelt impulse towards a
neighbour is already an assimilation of the mind of
Christ, and as such a *votum implicitum* of membership of the Church. It is a pulse of that Christ-life
which brings the whole of evolution and humanity's
obstinate upward struggle into the final event of conclusive advance, Christ's exodus, the resurrection.
Consequently Christians are people who, as Paul puts
it, bear in them the dynamic power of the resurrection, who have entered into communion with Christ's
sufferings and reproduce in their lives the pattern of
his death, in other words, people who hope. They can
truly be considered to attain the resurrection from the
dead. All these human beings are members of the
Church, the redemptive advance guard of the universe, whether they explicitly realize this or exercise
their membership in a way which is not yet articu-
lated in biblical ideas and terminology.

In this sense the theological statement that *Extra
ecclesiam nulla salus* (there is no salvation outside the
Church) is one of the most liberating messages in
Christian doctrine. If this proposition is examined in
accordance with the most elementary rules of logic, it

can be read in a way which is no longer depressing or scandalous but profoundly liberating. A universal negative proposition can in fact be converted into an equivalent positive statement. It can therefore just as well be said that wherever there is salvation, there is the Church (*ubi salus, ibi ecclesia*). In this sense this much-criticized doctrine is a splendid affirmation of freedom. It is surely a liberating thought that the Church is in fact present wherever a human being honestly strives for what is true and good, sacrifices himself in the hope of something greater, spends himself in service of his neighbour, dedicates himself wholly to a cause? In all these cases salvation is effected and the Church is present, perhaps to a greater degree than we dare to think, in lives which are perhaps more genuinely Christian than we are willing to suppose or admit.

Finally, we must raise the question how and by what standard the individual Christian can gauge the genuineness of the hope he has conceived. What criterion can we employ to estimate the sincerity and uprightness which gives our actions and reflections an eternal value?

In view of what has been said so far, martyrdom must surely be regarded as a criterion, and in fact in the concrete the only valid one. We must be grateful to Hans Urs von Balthasar for insistently drawing attention to this essential aspect of Christian life in his *Cordula oder der Ernstfall*, which, though of course a polemical work, goes for the essential. Christian reflection is always decided by reference to the testimony of blood. Only something that I can give my life for—it need not mean actual death, perhaps only the daily wear and tear of ordinary service of others, or the vocation to failure—is my central conviction, with an eternal value in my finite existence, prayer and reflection. No Christian is called to reflect on all mysteries, to utter all the prayers of the Church, to achieve everything with the same urgency. He has the right and duty to enter more deeply into the mystery at the particular points where he hears a special call to self-dedication. This will then constitute his own particular grace-given, charismatic personal life, his *theologia orans,* his prayerful thought. Say this, think that out, plunge into whatever it is that you would wish to save at the cost of your very life, for eternal fulfilment in the realm of hope come true. But accomplish it with the mind of Christ, the attitude of the martyr—defencelessly. Defencelessness is essential, the will not to strike back and triumph. It is a matter of those few last words that fell from the parched and tortured mouth of Christ on the cross. Non-retaliation, non-resistance, quiet detachment from the world, mark the depth of an unconditionally Christian life in its maturity. It is an attitude which all too often is condemned to defeat in the world, but it is the foundation on which our eternal home, heaven, will rise. It is in this spirit and with these principles that the Christian should meditate on the mysteries of his faith. Then perhaps he will appreciate in a unique way the beauty of Ignatius of Antioch's words in his letter to his brethren in Rome. "Now that I am a prisoner, I am learning to desire nothing. I am seeking him who died for me. I wish for him who rose for our sake. Birth awaits me. Let me receive pure light! When I arrive there I shall at last be a man. Grant that I may imitate the suffering of my God. Anyone who bears him within himself will understand what I desire, and will pray for me so that I may pass over to him." That is the theology of hope embodied in the testimony of a life.

This attitude has nothing to do with fanatical other-worldliness. Quite the contrary. Without an attitude of this kind it is not possible to take the world really seriously. The Christian has to be convinced that in one ultimate respect his earthly life is unimportant, and that an eternally enduring state of happiness and joy follows this life. He lives in dependence on a God beyond the world who is at the same time his constant quest. In hope, that is, by the deepest desire of his life, he has already arrived there. Nothing can therefore shake his mind. Here below he has no abiding city. Christ has taken his life with him. But this very detachment from the world is the reason why the same Christian must enter into the world, so thoroughly in fact that he almost forgets heaven in the process. For what is really decisive in the world is what is done without regard for reputation, success and self-righteousness, in other words, what is done purely out of human kindness and goodness. God is greater than all, but precisely for that reason he can be found everywhere, even in the most insignificant things. He can be met with on all the roads of the world. Such an attitude produces constant readiness to discern God's call in every situation in the world, a radical ability to serve our neighbour, and openheartedness towards all that is and lives. The Christian must seek his great God everywhere, even in the slightest things. Of course he must have the courage to be dissatisfied. It is his duty to have no abiding city except the unresting journey towards God's peace. Nothing but God is enough for him. His life here on earth and hereafter in eternity is a never-ending advance into what has no limits. Any fulfilment is only the beginning of further search. Even the greatest, most beautiful and holiest is not great, beautiful and holy enough for him. To express it paradoxically, he will not let himself be cramped by anything great. His desire and hope is always greater than the greatest achievement.

On the other hand, however, the Christian has as it were to conceal the vastness of his aspiration in the pettiness of earthly achievement. He must be able to use everything, even the most inadequate means, if he can serve God thereby. His hope is always open to what is higher and greater. The full measure of his life is measurelessness. Nevertheless his hope has to remain within the narrow bounds of what can be attained on earth. Anyone who can achieve measurelessness in great things and accept narrow limits in small embodies Christian hope in his own human reality. "Not to be cramped by the greatest, yet to accept the narrowest limits" would be an accurate summary of Christian thought and conduct of life. Calm amid unresting activity, peace amid agitation, acceptance of one's own limitations but constant and unlimited aspiration, contentment with the most insignficant, and continual striving for the more perfect—such is the attitude which Christ's own life exemplified as the fundamental law of Christian holiness. The whole tension between heaven and earth is summed up in a human being of this kind.

The Testing of Hope

CHRISTIANITY is the belief that with Christ's resurrection the destiny of the world is already decided. We are inescapably moving towards heaven because wittingly or unwittingly we exist as Christians, that is, "in Christ." In all the provisional things of the world, the final and definitive is already at work. No search peters out in vacuity. "Nothing can separate us from the love of Christ." Nothing except the rejection of that very love itself. We have finally arrived at freedom, open and joyous. "I have set before you an open door which no one is able to shut," Christ says in the Book of Revelation (3:8). Wherever a flame of hope still burns, however low, the light of heaven is already visible. No aspiration is disappointed. We lose nothing, least of all what we renounce in our lifetime. In a world of this kind there is no reason for despair and faintheartedness. The Christian is "born to a living hope." This imposes the Christian obligation that the one life we have on earth must be "successful," so that through us humanity and the world may have more light and perfection. Each is responsible by his life for the happiness of the world.

"Success in being human" is what traditional theology called "virtue." Virtue does not mean mere decency, honesty or dull respectability. On the contrary, it is the most explosive thing imaginable in the world. It is diametrically opposed to what the word suggests in everyday usage, which makes it sound so lacking in style, so tasteless and philistine. In reality it means the full realization of human capacity for existence. It means a fulfilment which does not occur merely sporadically, as occasion offers, but one which decisively affects human life and constantly directs it towards essentials. Virtue is therefore the most unconventional and unlikely thing we can come across in our world—genuine human reality achieved by personal effort and lived as testimony. It is of course expressed in individual actions, but it essentially consists in disposition and intention. It is the deep current of an individual destiny, involving breadth and sensitivity of feeling, knowledge and decision. In a "virtuous" human being something would be operative which Aquinas describes by the strange expression "*opinio vehemens*"—a heightened, incisive and concentrated force of vital activity. His existence would be ardent and glowing in its transparency to the ground of all that exists.

This exemplary transparency in personal life springs from unselfishness, which is the measure and criterion of all virtuous human activity and of all life in hope. It means kindness of heart won by self-mastery, distinction and delicacy in personal relationships, sensitivity to the greatness in others. An attitude of this kind is found only in human beings whose vital concerns are not solely for themselves, and whose lives and experiences are centred primarily on others, not on their own ego. Such a person masters himself and gives himself, seeking disinterestedness, availability.

He no longer has an eye to himself, but sets himself to serve his brethren. The profoundest and most authentic selfhood is therefore unselfishness. It also includes that receptivity which Christ in his unforgettable summons called poverty in spirit. At the end of life this alone can hold out absolutely empty hands to God and receive perfect fulfilment, heaven as an unmerited gift.

This unobtrusive attitude of hope, which raises human and mundane reality towards heavenly fulfilment, and which, we have seen, essentially consists in an unselfishness that has become second nature, is vulnerable. It is endangered less perhaps by individual acts of revolt, by particular sins, than by a more fundamental threat, a strange and almost imperceptible drift into inauthenticity, which for our purpose we might tentatively call a sinful way of living life itself.

A human being gradually becomes impenetrable and hard, rigid and unreceptive. At every small step into the abyss he can say it is justifiable, good and even a Christian duty to do what he is doing. Nevertheless in this process of inner collapse a human being comes into existence who is satisfied with himself, his successes and habits, who devotes himself to his own concerns, who can no longer dream of any greater fulfilment, who is continually worried whether he is losing or gaining something, who is no longer capable of self-giving. Life without hope. This condition of living darkness can come about without any identifiable grave sin. This sinful way of living life has nothing dramatic or promethean about it. It merely consists of petty egotism in everyday affairs, damaging spite, rash judgment, impatience, insensitivity in personal relationships, inability really to listen to others, to allow them to express themselves as they really are, resentment, lack of respect for the inner life of others, moodiness, waste of time, spiritual inertia. All this and much more would have to be taken into account if we were to speak about this sinful way of living life, the sin of hopelessness. It is sometimes too exacting, demands too much effort, to commit a grave sin. There are situations in life, times of low ebb, in which people cannot bring themselves to the point of fully committing themselves, of translating their fundamental inner decision into action, outwardly express their total commitment. Yet they have perhaps already failed in God's sight, fundamentally, because the whole life they are living is a lie, a total collapse, without hope and radiating no hope to anyone else.

If we try to draw out the theological implications of all this, the vital significance of well-worn terms such as "purgatory" and "judgment" comes home to us more forcefully.

Purgatory. At death, all the inauthenticity and hopelessness that a man has accumulated within him collapses. He is confronted with what he really is and what that reality of his amounts to in eternal values. His success is in ruins, his power ebbs away, his wealth evaporates. In the flame of Christ's love our life will take fire. No one can endure the full realization of hope, heaven, in his earthly fragility. Not even God can transport him into heaven unpurified. The experience of heaven would destroy him. At death, however, Christ affords us a last opportunity—for many it is their first—to imitate his disposition, to become perfectly sincere. Man has no longer any external support. His whole existence depends on those remnants to which his own reality is now reduced—his longing, his cry for help, his helpless abandonment to absolute mercy. Then man recognizes that in reality he never was, and is now left with, anything more than his renunciation, his hope and his unselfishness: patient hours with a suffering friend, experiences of sincerely devoted love and friendship, the happiness of not belonging to oneself, the will to mourn with those who mourn and rejoice with those who rejoice, in short, to be a source of hope for the hopeless. The final reduction of a human being to the essential of his disposition, to hope, to his capacity for what is great, is precisely what purgatory is. It is a frequent experience of all lovers to be humbled by love, and this is what happens in death.

A human being cannot be wholly himself in this way, however, without at the same time experiencing through his own "humanization" the reality of the incarnate Lord. Consequently man's meeting with himself in death (purgatory) becomes a meeting with God in Christ (judgment). By knowing himself with complete honesty, man comes to know Christ. In this sense the judgment will be the most matter of fact and at the same time the most surprising thing in our existence: the revelation of the hidden Christ-dimension of the hope which we gave others. In Matthew's Gospel the just (and also the unjust) ask Christ, "Lord, when did we do this to you?" When did we see him hungry, thirsty, naked, sick, a stranger, in prison? They obviously performed the greatest actions of their lives without really realizing what they were doing. The judgment will bring to light a dimension of our earthly actions, however ephemeral they may seem in our experience, which leads directly to Christ. It will show the ultimate sense of our experiences, of our aspirations, of our longing for greatness, friendship and kindness, of our hope. Nothing else matters; it all falls away, no longer forming any obstacle to prevent a man from entering into absolute joy.

The fundamental meaning of purgatory and judgment can therefore be understood in the following way.

Heaven is only endurable to those who have the courage to give hope to themselves and their brethren by loving action, that is, by unselfishness. Purgatory and the judgment take place in the flame of God's love. God cannot judge anyone. His very nature consists purely of love, of unselfish affection. Despite his omnipotence, God is incapable of exiting any creature from himself. He always and everywhere lovingly welcomes his creature. Consequently the judgment can only be understood as man's self-judgment in the light of his hope and the love of God.

Purgatory and judgment are not mythical events, they are hope unfolding to its final conclusion, the longing of the human heart for goodness, truth and radiant being. What takes place in them is a total activation of that disposition which medieval theology recognized to be the fundamental attitude of the human soul: the "restlessness of the heart" which causes man to go forward into the future in anticipation and expectation. In purgatory and judgment a final and definitive conversion of attitude takes place, a turning to the essential. To achieve this even tentatively in this present life, among provisional earthly things, is precisely what constitutes the testimony of a Christian life of hope.

The logic of Christian hope is inescapable. Genuine human reality is found in hope; hope takes place in self-sacrifice; sacrifice means self-forgetfulness; self-forgetfulness is accomplished by renunciation; selfless renunciation is already love; love is akin to God; from the closeness to God attained by love, there arises a new world, heaven. To live in hope means, in concrete terms, to sacrifice self without bitterness, to renounce superficial self-fulfilment in order to be close to others, to be able to bring the light of hope to all.

By his hope, his innermost longing and endeavour, man is perpetually living with limitless vistas. A great lack of moderation is second nature to him and constantly impels him. The more definitely a man hopes, the more human he is. Nevertheless there is another aspect, for, as Paschasius Radbertus has admirably expressed it, "Reverent fear guards the summit of hope." And in the Old Testament it is said, in simple yet sublime words, "They that hope in the Lord shall fear him." Man's hope leads to fear. Fear and uncertainty remind him that although human existence is disposed and directed towards fulfilment by the highest conceivable reality, in fact by a reality which transcends all thought, it is nevertheless vulnerable. We are always merely advancing towards hope, and can lose it. We are vulnerable because we are commonplace and everyday. Our dreams are uncertain. We cannot look forward freely, sense what really matters and accept it disinterestedly.

At what point in human life does temptation against hope concentrate? What is the origin of that darkening of reality that shuts out Christ and offers God no lodging? And on the other hand, what victory brings the Christian to the fullness of the promise? From the point of view of theology and of a philosophy of man, the most important New Testament text on these questions is the account of Christ's temptations. The question whether the Gospel story of the temptation in the desert is to be regarded as the representation of an historical event or rather as an interpretation of Christ's moral disposition by the primitive Church (or perhaps as both event and interpretation), cannot be answered in clear-cut terms. But even on the assumption that it is a purely theological interpretation of Christ's personal life by the primitive community, it is still the case that Christ's friends knew he had saved our human reality from extreme distress. This distress is signified by the image of the wilderness. To go out into the desert means to expose oneself to the uncanny, to encounter danger, to attack evil in its own realm, in the abode of the demons. What is this abode of the evil one like, this dwelling of hopelessness? We find in the account of the three temptations of Christ in the desert, three clues by which to sketch the temptations to which human hope is liable.

Success. Led by the Spirit, Christ leaves human security behind him. He flees the crowd. He goes to the extreme. He fasts for forty days and forty nights; he goes to the limit of what is humanly endurable. Then he feels a radical hunger. Perhaps not so much for food as for human company. Then a tremendous temptation befalls him. What if he were to change stones into bread? This temptation wants Christ to externalize the power which makes him sincere and genuine, rooted in essential human reality, and which makes him the "author of life." The danger is great. Not only Christian life but unqualified human authenticity is at stake.

With the concentrated power of his divine and human existence, Christ accepts the hazard of being a sincere and genuine man, living from the heart, without double-dealing, or acting a part, but joining the ranks of the oppressed and the downtrodden, enduring the distress and powerlessness of being human. Here was a decision of inconceivable scope. The shadow world of apparent success was declared by

Christ to be futile, while longing, hope and, therefore, quiet unassuming love and friendship were established as the ultimate standard of Christian life. A human being had finally dared not to identify himself with a role assumed merely before others. Christ's choice was to live entirely in hope and intention, to exist in the inner truth of life and experience, with all that such an attitude involves in our world, sympathy, loneliness, doubt, anxiety for friends, even ultimate despair.

Christ's decision meant, therefore, changing men's hearts to unaffected goodness instead of stones into bread. By this he made it clear to us that we are more than anything we have attained and achieved in life, more than our success. Those who can no longer say that of themselves sincerely and with feeling, have succumbed to temptation against hope, even if they have been very successful in the struggle against specifically recognizable sins.

Thirst for power. The account of Christ's second temptation leads us even deeper into the vulnerability of hope and the promise it holds. A bewildering vertigo fills Christ's soul. In spirit he stands on the pinnacle of the Temple, sees the steep fall, the abyss, the swarming crowds. "Throw thyself down, nothing can hurt thee!" The Messiah is to be exceptional. He is to come down from above, unexpectedly, startling and impressive. The tempter wanted to cause the greatest event of human reality, God's incarnation, to be revealed to the crowds of people down there dreaming of a ruler, by a bold stroke, an act of force, thus ensuring that it would be inwardly corrupted and outwardly misunderstood. Redemption as self-glorification. Once again what is at stake is the very essence of human reality.

Christ did not want the exceptional. He did not wish to be borne up by the hands of angels, did not wish not to strike his foot against a stone. He accepted for himself the frustration which every deeply human relationship—love, friendship, association—must pass through some time, and trod the way of the cross to the point of dereliction by God. He willed to be powerless. But the powerlessness of his humility was not a cramping or denial of reality, it was an affirmation of life. He wanted to give himself undividedly to all. Even to those who, like the tax-gatherer, are far from God and do not dare even to raise their eyes to heaven. Humility is a love which has grown to maturity. It is the extra, the *"plus et ego"* of affirmation of life, of giving in hope. Anyone who loves will at some time in his life come to a limit where he will have to accept humiliation. The whole love of his life will be put to the test then.

How powerless and helpless someone can be whose love is of that quality! He renounces his own power, submits to another's destiny, which he tries to protect and defend, tries to answer for others, to endure and help to bear another's weakness, share his happiness and misfortune. To be at another's call, open and sensitive to other people's distress, to accept their lives unreservedly—these are marks by which we recognize the inner power but also the powerlessness of a love which is a source of hope to others. Our inner revolt against the gravity, the human impossibility of fulfilment and the humility of love, explains the significance of Christ's second temptation.

Wealth. Christ's third temptation represents the conclusive, irrevocable victory of the redeemer over the power of the evil one. At the same time it leads into the deepest threat to human hope. Christ is "taken up to a very high mountain," sees all the kingdoms of the world and their glory. He feels he is in a vast space, a different kind of space. A feeling of liberation wells up in his soul. His mind experiences the power of comprehension, possession, mastery. Yet Christ rejects even this feeling as a temptation. The whole world lay at his feet. He came down from this exalted feeling into the wretchedness of human life, the company of simple people, the dust and weariness of our existence. He chose to live in the world of the poor and to show what love can achieve when it dares to be total and unmixed. He willed to be a witness of unconditional risk, patience and achievement, to bear witness to hope. That was Christ's manner of life, to be there for others, unconditionally; to be exposed to the immediate impact of the moment and the human distress of all kinds which it reveals. His life was dominated by respect for others' personal life and by creative presence.

The attitude of poverty of spirit is the mode of life of those who have attained interior freedom. They may possess this world's goods but they are not possessed by them. Quiet and unaffected practice of the truth. Nothing spectacular. No extraordinary personality on the scene. The person in question steps back, becomes unnoticeable. Simplicity, responsibility, detachment from self-satisfaction, self-conquest and serenity prevail. Under the heavy pressure of the world a human being takes shape who has found in hope a way to devote himself to God. What does this poverty of Christ mean for our Christian life?

The new man, truly established in Christ, ought to endeavour to share the lot of the poor and hopeless. What is decisive here is the will to self-sacrifice. A person of this sort will not perhaps achieve very much in the world, but his existence is a special grace for others. He does not mind drab everyday routine. He no longer wants to be his own master. A human being who is really good, whose intentions are good, spontaneously makes a gift of himself. To give oneself, to give away what has been acquired and possessed is the characteristic mark of the good. But that is not the entire truth. Christ has loved us even more. He created us for a personal response. He begs for our answer, our love. God has visited us. He became appallingly weary, that is why he sat down by Jacob's Well in the blazing heat of noon. To all of us he will appear one day at death, like that, like a beggar. He will stand there, kind, full of understanding and defenceless in the blinding clarity of his love. The Christian, too, is a beggar, should be a beggar. God wants his love to take the form of powerlessness, humility and poverty. To what unselfishness God is leading us! What a shining sign of hope he wants to set up in us!

The attitude achieved through Christ's temptation in the desert—the choice of inwardness, powerlessness and spiritual poverty—produced a radiant existence. Christ went to face chaos. He was equipped only with readiness for total self-sacrifice. In the desert his life shone like a torch. The world became light, opened out to the light. The framework of meaningless things collapsed and the true nature of things, heaven, unfolded. A Christian who tries to acquire this attitude without haste or selfish rigidity, but with serene simplicity in his everyday life, will be happy in the service of God. He has given hope to life. He has conquered despair in his own life.

Suffering in Hope

AT this point we should like to raise a question which is one of the most torturing problems of human existence. How is the Christian to come to terms with suffering? The mystery of suffering presents a profound challenge to Christian thought, prayer, inquiry and silence. The harsh reality of suffering cannot be argued away in a superficial way. The answer itself must be suffered, form part of our own suffering. "Tell me what you think of suffering and I will tell you who you are"—and also—"how much you yourself have suffered!" Reflection on human suffering discloses the real depths of human reality and the conduct of life. Christianity's answer to our present question has various levels. To distinguish them correctly, two main considerations must be taken into account.

The fundamental and all-pervasive Christian attitude to life, and therefore to suffering, is hope, or, in even more concrete terms, joy in existence. This is perhaps the most difficult task enjoined on a believer as testimony to life. Joy, however, is the *spiritus principalis,* the dominant spirit of Christian life, the spirit of the good news. For the earliest Christian community Christ was the author of life, the firstborn from the dead, the beginning of the new creation, the first-fruits, the ground of the new world. In these to some extent forgotten New Testament titles of the redeemer, Christ appears as the prince of life, as it were as the pilot of the whole creation, the spear-head of universal development. This cosmic position of Christ gives rise in the realm of Christian sensibility (in the Christian soul) to reverence for all that is, respect for life, sympathy with every creature, universal benevolence. Life can no longer fail now that Christ has risen. It has been definitively established in the transfigured body of the redeemer. It has become infinitely precious, and reserved for eternal fulfilment. There is an ultimate depth in each creature, which is already a heavenly dimension. The experiences of suffering and death also have to be integrated into this fundamental attitude of all-pervasive joy, if they are to be thought out and come to terms with in a Christian way.

This delight in existence produces in the Christian a tranquil, noble serenity which finds its valid expression in the term "providence." "We know that everything works for good with those who love God" is how the Letter to the Romans formulates the essential content of the Christian conception of providence. Providence is not a sentimental consolation in dream and fantasy. The Christian does not regard himself as specially favoured, a "Sunday's child." Fundamentally, providence consists in the fact that God loves us. This means that my life is never alien and remote from God. There is no situation from which I cannot find my way to God. My whole existence, whatever happens, is open to God in all its aspects. There is no entanglement, no suffering, no death, no sin, which God's love cannot turn into an occasion of grace. The promise of the Book of Revelation is addressed to all of us. "I have set before you an open door, which no one is able to shut." Certainly Christ's grace does not make life easy. After all, we did not become Christians to simplify things. The Christian finds himself in the same world as everyone else, embedded in it, bound by its laws and dependent on its conditions. He suffers, struggles and dies like any other man. But suffering, conflict and death can assume a different, new meaning for him, one of promise and hope. Faith is no quack's stall where everything can be had on the cheap as though by magic. Everything remains where it was, fixed, perhaps immovable. Nevertheless in this rigid reality a new possibility of understanding, endurance and patience opens out. How does this happen?

This is the anxious question of any Christian who honestly tries to practise his hopeful and joyful faith in a world torn by suffering. We have a right to ask this question. Mary first asked it. She put it urgently to the angel of the Annunciation in similar terms. *"Quomodo fiet istud?*—How can this be?" If we are not mistaken, Christianity has three answers of differing depth and significance to the question of how the Christian can change suffering into hope.

The first of these is by sympathy. Through the suffering of our brethren, God moves us in the very core and root of our own being, and arouses mercy in us. A merciful man has a heart for the misfortune, misery and distress of other people. When charity has become deeply rooted in a human being, suffering immediately makes its home with him. People notice unselfishness and sympathy remarkably quickly. They seek help and, more than anything, human affection from such selfless charity. The hungry seek food, the thirsty drink, the naked clothing, strangers a home, prisoners their freedom, the sick assistance, and the dying support. This is the usual way the Christian doctrine of man describes the seven works of mercy, simply but nobly. The whole range of human distress is visible in them.

To take this distress upon ourselves entails suffering, sometimes intolerably grave suffering. Other people's troubles wear us out more than our own. Our existence is more vulnerable to other people's frailty than to our own. Often the helplessness of the compassionate is crushing. People come to us with faces ravaged by suffering and we are powerless to help. Every possibility may have been exhausted, every resistance offered to all the bodily and mental pain in the world which deserves to be eradicated and destroyed. Yet with some kinds of profound suffering all that remains possible is to share the suffering by sympathy, to open one's heart and allow the other's suffering to fill it, persevering until the sufferer feels buoyed up by having someone to feel and bear his pain with him. Then the compassionate has served as grace of comfort from God, a witness of hope for the sufferer. We must therefore try to look further into the mystery of compassion.

A Christianity which evades the urgent demands of love for the poorest, the deserted and the hopeless has abandoned its essence. To be a Christian in this respect means to be deeply moved by God through the sufferings of my brethren. I have to help my lonely and suffering brother, that is how I am a Christian.

We must look at this question of coming to terms with suffering by sympathy even more closely. Who is this neighbour that I have to help if I am to be worthy of the name of Christian at all? When Christ was

asked about this he did not give an abstract definition
but told the parable of the good Samaritan. What it
says might be summarized as follows. My neighbour
is anyone who has only me to help him. He is my
neighbour if without me he would have nowhere in
the world to turn. If I do not help him, no one else
will? Then he is my neighbour. The whole Christian
attitude to life is summed up in this parable. Do what
no one else can or will do in your place. Be ready.
Cultivate openheartedness on principle, and be aware
of suffering. Then sometime you will meet someone
who has no one else to turn to but you. It is their lot
you will have to shoulder. You must stop. You cannot
pass by. It is the human being who stoops to his
brother in need who is a Christian, whether he has
yet heard of God or Christ or not. God's creative mark
since the beginning of the world has been to shelter,
to protect, to ward off injuries, to bind up wounds.
The more we oppose our neighbour's suffering with
all our powers, the nearer we come to the heart of
God and the more light and hope there is in our
world. Compassion is the atmosphere of feeling and
action which infuses hope and life into our brethren.
What demands compassion can make on a man can
be seen from an incident reported in the Gospel of St
John: ". . . Jesus went up to Jerusalem. Now there is
in Jerusalem by the Sheep Gate a pool, in Hebrew
called Beth-zatha, which has five porticoes. In these
lay a multitude of invalids, blind, lame, paralysed.
One man was there, who had been ill for thirty-eight
years. When Jesus saw him and knew that he had
been lying there a long time, he said to him, 'Do you
want to be healed?' The sick man answered him, 'Sir, I
have no man to put me into the pool when the water
is troubled, and while I am going another steps down

before me.' Jesus said to him, 'Rise, take up your pallet, and walk.' And at once the man was healed, and he took up his pallet and walked" (5:1-9).

This account brings us to the essence of Christian compassion. It is one of the most terrible experiences in life to have to lament that "I have no one." What the sufferer wants most of all in fact is not help but a companion. As long as anyone around us, in the circle of people with whom we are in touch, has to say "I have no one," we are not genuine Christians. To the compassionate, every stranger, outcast and homeless person is a friend. He feels what suffering means to the sufferer, the oppression, the darkness, the hopelessness, that oppress him. Charity, the essential act of Christian life, means willingness to form and maintain a truly personal association, active and faithful whatever the suffering, until death. That is why only such love can console.

The consoler must become the sufferer himself if he is to understand him at all, and it is love that produces such identity. Then if he attempts words of consolation they do not come from outside, as it were, but from within, welling up in the soul of the sufferer himself. Then it is no longer merely "suffering" that is being talked about, but "your suffering" which through mutual affection has become mine. But anyone who risks offering consolation by real sympathy of this sort, will have to take the consequences of his dedication by renewing again and again his "creative presence," forging that stern tie which wears away our very life itself, and which we call fidelity. Suffering is fully suffering only when it stretches out over whole expanses of time. That is when it exerts its full power to destroy. That is when it starts to poison the very springs of life and to crush the inmost fibres. To share the experience of a slow, long drawn-out disintegration of a human life by suffering, and by doing so constantly to renew and provide for it a "creative presence," is probably the hardest demand made on us by the fact that we are Christians. Such fidelity goes far beyond the limits of what is humanly to be expected. It amounts in fact to the presence of the absolute goodness of God in our dark world, the presence of heaven in the domain of suffering. The human being to whom God sends someone to whom he can and may show compassion, must certainly be called fortunate. He has been chosen by God to live up to the vocation of total self-sacrifice, keeping hope alive in humanity, and of radiating Christian joy by the witness of his own life.

The second kind of transformation of suffering into hope is known to the Christian idea of man as sacrifice. What does the Christian vocation of a suffering human being consist in? How is he to come to terms in a Christian way with his own distress? Pierre Teilhard de Chardin, who knew by personal experience a great deal about affliction, sickness, failure and mental and physical collapse, wrote a preface to the Notebooks of his invalid sister. In it we read, "O Marguerite, my sister, while I, in my devotion to the positive forces of the universe, was roaming over continents and oceans, you, stretched out motionless on your bed of sickness, were silently transforming into light the most grievous shadows of the world. Tell me, in the eyes of the creator, which of us will have chosen the better part?"*

The Christian has the task of overcoming the darkness of the world, of bringing light and joy into the

* *Teilhard de Chardin, A Guide to His Thoughts*, E. Rideau, Collins 1967, p. 298.

world. Every Christian has this vocation. The world
is full of gloom, confusion and obscurity. If a Christian
receives the great grace of God to combine these kinds
of darkness in his own life, and to endure them pa-
tiently, he can be sure he has been specially chosen to
bear witness to joy. God has destined him to concentrate in himself the burdens, darkness and weight of
the world and to transform them into God's joy. If he
does so, his own soul will be increasingly darkened
by suffering, but the world around him will become
clearer and more serene. By bearing the obscurity and
gloom of the earth in his own person, but at the same
time opening his own darkness to the light of Christ,
he has made the world happier and brought it a little
nearer to heaven. To bear in Christian sacrifice the
mental and physical distress of humanity reduces the
level of suffering in the whole world. Those who understand this do not need to be told anything more
about the mystery of human suffering. They will even
have the courage to thank God for their suffering.
They will understand that God has chosen them to
endure what others are no longer able to bear. The
sick who suffer in a Christian spirit are our deliverers;
they make it possible for us to live in light and give
ourselves up to joy.

Perhaps the line of thought we have been tracing
is not immediately intelligible to everyone. We shall
therefore try to supplement it with something simpler.
A man can come to realize that his own suffering is a
powerful motive, and can come to his full maturity
through it. Human life does not run on the same plane
throughout its course. Its structure is related to its
culminating meaning. There are various stages on the
one road of life. On the higher level, different patterns

of meaning prevail. Søren Kierkegaard, the Danish philosopher and theologian, expressed this particularly clearly in his work *Stages on Life's Road*. Man only attains the higher stage of human life by allowing himself, in a crisis of his whole personal existence, to be forced out of the realm of what he has experienced and achieved so far, by making a decision and staking his soul. Human reality authentically lived takes shape on different existential levels according to the hazards which have to be confronted at each stage. St Augustine, for example, was compelled by the death of a young friend to take the decisive leap which changed his life. The Buddha, as a young prince, in a single flash of spiritual insight realized the suffering of the world. He stood up, we are told, and went out into homelessness. Often it is an illness or the collapse of a life's work or the deeply-felt departure of someone to whom we are attached which gives the decisive impetus to this leap into the dark, into the unexplored. In certain circumstances this may even apply to sin. In view of the sinners who have become saints, an Augustine, a Magdalen, a Lydwina, we have no hesitation in saying *"felix culpa."* Not because the sin itself was no sin, but because it drove a human being into the arms of God. Human suffering, bodily pain and even the evil of sin were simply means to tear us from ourselves, to detach us from our successes, to make a real person of us. When some grief, shock, pain, compels us to rise to a higher plane of personal life, we must admit that they were in the service of life and hope. If we never lived through such times of mental and physical crisis our life would stagnate.

From the two lines of thought we have been considering, we might well note the following. Human life only progresses, rises higher, if it is forced out of the stage it has reached and ventures to break out of its petty limits. It is in suffering and pain that man realizes that he is not simply himself, that he has to achieve his own identity, that he is a hope. In suffering we learn that our real self has not yet been found, that we are still on the way. In order really to be able to live, one must have despaired of life at some time or another. God preserve us from those people who have always succeeded in life, who have never had to cry out in despair, who have never felt the apparent meaninglessness and fragility of human life through some illness which sapped them to the utmost or some choking distress of mind, who have never begged and prayed the Lord to free them at last from their suffering by death and to take them to heaven. Such people have not yet realized the blessedness in that cry of hope in the last words of holy Scripture, "Come, Lord Jesus!" What hope would there be for our world if no human could utter any longer this advent cry for eternal fulfilment?

Finally the third and highest possible way of coming to terms with human suffering must be considered. We have to take a step further, in which the ground gives way completely beneath us, the step to dereliction. There is human suffering—death above all is of this kind—in which man arrives at an absolute limit. The secure framework of human reality collapses. Man can no longer master his suffering. He can no longer come to terms with his own destiny. He cries out, "My God, why hast thou forsaken me?" In such moments even the presence of God is experienced as dereliction. From collapse to collapse man has crumbled to dust. Nothing is left of him but his weariness. He is too stricken to live, too restless to die. The terrible thing is, he thinks he no longer loves God, thinks he does

not even want to love him any more. Is there still any
answer, any hope in this case? Yes. God is the wholly
other. And the wholly other begins where we cease
to be. We can only meet him at the end of our strength.
Perhaps only in what to the eyes of the world seems
foolish, intolerable to the feelings and meaningless
to the understanding. Only in radical humiliation,
dereliction, defeat, is man confronted with what is
radically great, the Absolute. We should take good
care not to deprive a suffering human being of this
precious gift by our pious chatter, bemusing him with
our superficial arguments until he can no longer experience his own dereliction. That would mean that
no one would experience God's total otherness any
longer, and that no one would be able to receive
God's total gift. If it is to share in the wholly other,
every human life must come to this most intolerable
of sufferings. That is when the world opens out on to
limitless transcendence, in which a new world takes
shape, not by human power but by the powerlessness
of the cross, which draws down the power of God.

Here once again there appears to be a possible approach to a more intimate understanding of death.
During our earthly life we are still travelling far from
authentic reality, in fact we constantly pass God by.
We are dominated by people, things and events, by
our longings and dreams. These fill the whole horizon
within and without, and hold us in their grip. Such
a multiplicity of things leaves practically no room for
God in our minds. When a human being is to enter
heaven, where all hopes are fulfilled, he must have
one chance, in death, of experiencing total dereliction
and thus knowing God with dazzling clarity. Until
then, man could confuse God with something else,
with his own desires, his sense of life, his instinctive

joy in the beautiful and good. But when there is nothing else left of a man, God is there, purely and simply God. A man can at last die into God. This means he must be stripped of everything to which he clings with every fibre of his being, his things, his possessions, his dreams, everything that he has built up and achieved in this life. By experiencing death, man is freed from all that had hindered him from looking God in the face. In death, man is totally delivered up to God. Christ himself had to take upon himself the agony of dereliction and death, in order that every human being who goes the way of deprivation may be able in death to meet him with dazzling clarity, and so that every human being, at least in death, may know him with every fibre of his very self and so be able to make a free and final decision about him. Death opens up absolute hope.

We have not answered the question of suffering. Humanly speaking it is unanswerable. We could only give a few pointers on how a Christian who is honestly living his faith can come to terms with suffering and transform it into hope, through sympathy, sacrifice and dereliction. The strange thing is that through these, the waves of suffering which flow through humanity from generation to generation come to break in foam on the shores of eternity.

The Future of Hope

In this meditation we want to try to take a decisive step towards the mystery of our hope, by thinking prayerfully about heaven. By way of introduction, however, a few preliminary ideas will have to be presented in an inevitably abstract way. Then perhaps in the later course of our meditation it may be easier to catch some glimpse of the serene and translucent beauty of heaven.

Human existence is driven in all essential respects by a hidden impulse. This lies behind man's "high aspiring mind;" it is the soul's urge and appetite for something great still to come. That is what the old thinkers used to call the *"extensio animi ad magna,"* and which we for our purpose might tentatively call basic hope. By its very structure human consciousness is turned towards the future. Our present moment is still obscure. What has only just been experienced is often least recoverable. There is no light at the foot of the lighthouse. What is approaching, however, the future, is sufficiently far away for the beam of consciousness to be able to focus on it. Human living, therefore, always involves the foretaste of something else. Expectation never dies down in us. People are always imagining new wishes for themselves. By his very nature man always sees light ahead, in what is not yet there. An indestructible instinct, in fact, impels man in the direction of a happy ending. This is not merely a case of the credulity of the masses. Hope of a better future is ineradicably grounded in the human desire for happiness. Now this latter is clearly the motive force driving all genuine human thought, creation, dreams and wishes. Man's "birth" is therefore still in progress until his death.

This basic hope of human existence takes shape in the Christian conception of man as expectation of heaven. The unknown always attracts men as something more beautiful and worthy of attainment. What people ultimately strive for and catch a glimpse of in the various reflections of their basic hope, is "home," the moment of fulfilment. That tempestuous scholastic Abelard said, "The goal is that community in which longing does not outrun reality, and where fulfilment in not inferior to longing." If it is true that man must be drawn to genuine humanity by the challenge of his future, and that he essentially transcends past and present in his still undiscovered essence, then the Christian idea of an absolute future, heaven, represents one of the most powerful motives of human life. Without heaven, earth would be humanly unlivable. Hopes and demands must be greater than the possibilities if reality is to be compelled to yield up all its possibilities and allow all its hidden springs to flow. That is why right down to the present day Christianity has taken human longing, man as dreamer, with the greatest seriousness. The absolutely unsurpassable pitch of ultimate fulfilment is magnificently expressed by St Paul in a basic principle of the Christian interpretation of life, "What no eye has seen, nor ear heard, nor the heart of man conceived, what God has prepared for those who love him." Even from this point of view Christianity is the religion which most truly corresponds to man's real nature. Consequently Christians feel a certain solidarity with all hope, even of a purely human kind. Anyone who speaks the language of hope is our brother. Wittingly or not, he bears within him the longing for a world exactly as it should be, that is, heaven. The thought of heaven is a matter of radical hope, and such hope is, as we have seen, absolutely central. Heaven is the most intensely meaningful focus of all the most vital longing of humanity.

There is good reason for astonishment at how few Christians are consciously affected by the thought of heaven. It is surely a disturbing symptom, for example, that quite a number of priests nowadays never preach about heaven. What is the cause of such strange indifference or inability? It is certainly not easy to announce "objectively" the Christian message of eternal life. To speak about heaven we have to deal, as we have just seen, with the ultimate mystery of human life, but this mystery inspires all our actions and desires. Speech can never be adequate to the innermost essence of hope or the transcendence of its goal. Nor is revelation itself, for while it speaks clearly about the fact of our eternal happiness, it is largely silent as regards the mode and manner of our fulfilment. Who is capable here on earth of describing what will happen at death when we meet the grace, friendship and beauty of God? We cannot speak adequately about heaven; we can, however, speak about our longing for it. On the other hand we also know that God, whom we long for, is holy. He is a God of those who hope, a God who spoke of himself under the image of a thoughtful and anxious host awaiting the arrival of his guests. God ready and waiting—the longing of the human heart. Is this not sufficient for us to outline a concrete practical theology of heaven, in touch with human concerns yet conscious with awe of the tremendous presence of the Absolute?

If we are to say something about heaven which is related to ordinary life and experience, we must first clear away misapprehensions which prevent our gazing into the light of God. The concept of immobility, for example, needs to be correctly understood. Our theology expresses the essential nature of heaven by the term beatific vision of God. Some theologians manage to make a masterpiece of boredom of this. The medieval scholastics, however, understood the word "vision" in the sense of holy Scripture. In the courts of oriental kings, "to see the king" was equivalent to "living in his presence." The mass of the people were not allowed to approach the king. They only caught sight of him on rare occasions, at a distance, enveloped in his splendour. Only trusted persons actually saw the king as he was. The difference was, therefore, that some knew whom they were seeing and meeting but remained essentially alien to him, whereas others were in direct contact with events and with the king in person. "To see God" really means, therefore, to share in his life, to enjoy his plenitude, to penetrate into the depths of his life, to be with him.

Similarly the expression "to know" in biblical usage does not denote a purely intellectual process, but the union of two beings in love. We read in Genesis, "Now Adam knew Eve his wife, and she conceived and bore a son." The union of two human beings in love of body and soul becomes an image of the knowledge that takes place in heaven between God and man, and which Christ regarded as the essence of eternal life.

Even these two brief examples make it clear how we must think about heaven. We may and must project our earthly experience, the most beautiful and un-alloyed experiences of our life, into a transcendent ful-filment which completes them by raising them to a higher order. We must think of human things and catch a glimpse of the divine through them. Since God's incarnation we have a right to the humaniza-tion of the divine. Heaven is not matter transformed into light, or a rigid, wooden stare at an external spectacle; it is rather an eternal production or even creation of the world through our eternal sharing in God's being. But anyone who realizes the fragility of human language and earthly feeling will exercise the greatest reserve in describing heaven. Only one person has given a proper account of heaven, and he came down from heaven, our Lord Jesus Christ. The theo-logian will therefore be well advised with courteous reserve to leave God himself to speak about heaven, and allow his own soul to be filled and inspired by the biblical symbols so that hope may return to his heart and his mind to take fire with love. "Only God speaks well of God," as Pascal says (*Pensées*, 799). Only Christ spoke well about heaven, as he spoke about eve-rything, directly and down-to-earth, quite simply, fa-miliarly and beautifully. What did he tell us about our eternal fulfilment?

Christ promised his own happiness to each. In order to give us some foretaste of the happiness of eternal union with God, Christ's revelation—whether in the gospels or in the Apocalypse—avoids any suggestion of sadness and depression. Heaven means absence of suffering. That is one of the constantly recurring themes of the New Testament in regard to eternal

glory. The elect are comforted, filled to satisfaction;
God himself will wipe every tear from their eyes.
There will be no more death, sadness or grief, pain
or tribulation. They will no longer hunger and thirst.
The sun will not burn them any more, nor any heat.
Those who have suffered persecution will possess
heaven. Revelation lists one image after another in order to bring home to us the unending happiness of being thus eternally showered with gifts, through the un-
complicated simplicity of human feeling. "It is done!
To the thirsty I will give water without price from
the fountain of life . . . I will be his God and he shall
be my son." Christ will confess the victor before his
Father and before his angels. The just will sit with
him on the throne of God. The blessed will receive
white garments and a crown; they will judge the
world; they will shine like the sun; God will give them
the morning star. They are all images of happiness,
purity, radiance and vitality, which the simplest understand yet which transcend the range of the expressible
by their profound symbolism. What theologian has
exploited to the full these images of enthronement
with God, judging the world, being sun and light,
wearing a crown of glory, possessing the morning star?

By way of supplement to these biblical metaphors
of eternal and perfect fulfilment, we shall quote a pas-
sage from Abbé Arminjon. St Thérèse of Lisieux, a
saint whose whole life was inspired by the close presence of heaven sensed by faith, received her first unforgettable impression of heaven when reading this
text:

> And God says, gratefully, Now it is my turn! How
> can I respond to the gift of themselves my friends
> have made except by giving myself without reserve?
> If I were to place in their hands the sceptre of crea-

tion, and were to clothe them with the radiance of my light, it would be a great deal, much more than they would have dared to wish for or to hope. But that would not be the ultimate impulse of my heart. I owe them more than Paradise, more than all the treasures of knowledge. I owe them my life, my essence, my eternal and infinite being. I must be the soul of their soul, pervading and filling it with my divinity, as the fire penetrates the glowing iron. By showing myself to them unveiled, I must unite myself with them in an eternal meeting face to face, so that my glory may illumine them, permeate them and radiate from every pore of their being, so that they may know me as I know them and they themselves become as gods.

This makes it clear that the gift of heaven is God himself, yet comes to us by means of creatures. "God will be all in all" for us. A God eternally serving! The inconceivable takes place. "Blessed are those servants whom the master finds awake when he comes; truly, I say to you, he will gird himself, and have them sit at table, and he will come and serve them." God himself becomes for us the place where reality is found. Not as though things, persons and events will cease to be themselves, but because God himself will come to us in them, in a thousand forms, and because he will raise their small finite reality by his powerful presence and make of them infinite gifts in finite form. All the gifts of happiness and of generous treatment flow to us wave upon wave in God's gift of himself. All pantheism is mere childish dreaming in comparison with this ultimate union of God with the creation, in which difference is not suppressed but the intimacy of the union increased.

Christ promised eternal life to each. Let us try quite

simply and without much system to advance further
into the divine promise, accepting the language of
revelation in its symbolical directness and without
transforming it into a thin, bloodless world of ideas,
a demythologized eternity. What does Christ in fact
promise us as heaven? He promised to a Samaritan
woman an everlasting spring of water, to the poor
people of Capharnaum the bread of eternal life, to
fishermen nets filled to bursting, to shepherds great
flocks and evergreen pastures, to merchants precious
pearls, to the farmer the prospect of unexpectedly
unearthing a treasure one day with his hoe, to the
Galilean peasants a hundredfold harvest. To us all he
promises an eternal wedding feast as a symbol of end-
less happiness in the company of the person we love.
The apostles promised the Greeks what pleased them
most—knowledge, learning, security in a spiritual city,
a radiant, translucent reality, built of shining jewels.
The Revelation to John evokes all the colours of the
world; precious stones are named, the voices of nature
ring out and enhance men's hymns of triumph; the
air is filled with perfumes rising from golden vessels.
On a white horse, accompanied by mounted troops,
he who is called "Faithful" and "True" appears. His
name is "The Word of God," "King of Kings." His robe
is dipped in blood. In a final battle he has saved our
nature for fulfilment. Now he celebrates the "wedding
feast of the lamb." From heaven a voice cries out,
"Behold, the dwelling of God is with men. He will
dwell with them, and they shall be his people, and
God himself will be with them."

To see what even now we can surmise is hidden,
to hear what even today can occasionally be heard
through the din of the world as if it were an earthly
echo from an eternal silence, to enter into contact

with what we have already felt in its earthly forms but
could never really hold—that is what heaven will be.
That inexpressible thing for which the Church prays
in the hymn to the Holy Spirit will take place:
"*Accende lumen sensibus.*" God's light will shine in
all our senses. Our whole being will be in contact with
God. Everything spiritual will enter into the sphere
of the senses, everything that belongs to the senses
will be included in the spirit, so that man in his unity
and totality will perceive and know all truth, which
is body and spirit, form and light, reality and meaning in one. "I shall make the victor a pillar in the
temple of my God. He will never lose his place there."
To be a pillar in God's temple means to act continually
to bear up the world, calmly and serenely with the
eternal vitality of unending existence. From these
metaphors we realize that direct contact with God
will bring us to total self-realization. Everything that
man has striven for in his lifetime, but only half
achieved, all that he could not be, what was hidden
from him, what failed, what was present only as a
still-born possibility, now blossoms into full reality.
His body becomes his very person, a perfect expression
of his inner being. A body formed by a new, unending power of the spirit. But since the deepest self-
realization always occurs as selflessness, in heaven the
whole person is dedicated to God and the brethren,
to liberation from self, forgetfulness of self in others.
It is clear that in heaven we shall find happiness less
in ourselves than in others. Those whom we have
loved in our lifetime will be heaven for us. Our beloved become an eternal happiness to us. Our mutual
love creates a new realm of reality. Heaven is the company of those we love developing into an eternal state
and increasingly close throughout eternity. We ex-

perience the warmth, radiance and life of the very essence of our beloved, who remain with us eternally, never to be lost. We shall always be at home in their love. Conversely, in us and through us heaven will come for others, for those we love; we make heaven, we become heaven for those whom we love. The earthly search for God, which at the same time is a preparation for heaven, is therefore the tenderest expression of my love for a human partner.

Christ promised us that we should become "as God." Jesus frequently describes eternal life as union with God. "If a man loves me, he will keep my word, and my Father will love him and we will come to him and make our home with him." "You shall eat and drink at table in my kingdom." "Behold, I stand at the door and knock. If anyone hears my voice and opens the door, I will come in to him and eat with him, and he with me. He who conquers, I will grant him to sit with me on my throne, as I myself conquered and sat down with my Father on his throne." God becomes my beloved for ever. Heaven is union but in distinction, without absorption or tedious uniformity. Duality remains, so that the happiness of union can be experienced all the more. As the Indian poet surprisingly says, "Not for itself is the water cool, but for the thirsty mouth. The pearl does not gleam for itself, but for the eye that admires it. How repugnant I find the doctrine that would fuse me with you into a single thing!" God creates love and is love. And love always means a Thou. The mystery of our divinization is that God is our Thou. The course of human love or friendship is an image of what happens to us in our love for God, an image of heaven. Human love itself produces a unity of being, a being together; the lovers receive themselves from one another as their mutual gift. Yet precisely for that reason they become even more of a person in themselves, an independent centre of loving affirmation. So in our love for Christ his reality becomes our own, although we do not on that account forfeit our own reality. But he is God. Something follows from this which we hardly dare to utter. In my loving affection I give myself to Christ and at the same time receive my life back from him, enriched with his own life. I become as Christ. I become the Son of the Father because Christ is the Son of the Father. My love for God is the same love with which he loves God: the Holy Spirit. Thus I am brought into the divine Trinity, veiled in mystery in earthly life, experienced clearly and totally in heaven. Behind my love for Christ, in the centre of my finite reality, the abyss of God opens out.

Let us try for a moment to forget the words "immortality," "ressurrection," "transfiguration of the world," even the word "heaven," and attempt to bring home to ourselves the essential element of our divinization, which we have only been able to express in stammered words, our being with God. Let us try to realize the mystery contained in the pregnant words of Christ's prayer at the Last Supper, "Father, the world has not known thee, and these know that thou hast sent me. I made known to them thy name, and I will make it known, that the love with which thou hast loved me may be in them, and I in them."

Man can save himself for eternity by love of God. This is his hope, his fundamental and ultimately decisive hope. Christ's resurrection inaugurated the "Last Days." In order to remain faithful to our vocation to love God, we must try to live even now as if we were already in heaven, as friends of Christ. Christ was never tired of speaking of this. Our destiny and our mission is love. Christ promised life to those who love, under various names and designations: Kingdom of heaven, country of the living, perfect consolation, fulfilment of our wishes, to be with God. He also pointed out the way there: detachment from ourselves, gentleness, human compassion, purity, peacemaking, hunger and thirst for justice (a world of goodness). All these things are essential characteristics of the love by which man receives himself, by giving himself. This is precisely what Christ taught.

If and because we are Christians, we have cause to rejoice here on earth. We feel, of course, how harsh and pitiless our life sometimes is, and how seldom our endeavours are crowned with success. Anxieties torment us. Failure and distress are our daily lot. God knows our suffering and he also knows that human suffering cannot be borne by any theoretical devices but only by hope. Hope does not take us out of the pain of time but makes it possible for us to accept the pain that belongs to time and to bear the cross of the present. A human being of this kind will be happy in the service of God and his brethren even if his life breaks down, even if he is a forlorn hope. He will stand up against the chaos that threatens the world, unconcerned whether in the end he will be left under its ruins. At the same time he will be very human: quiet, unassuming, always intervening at the point where the world threatens to sink back into loneliness and hopelessness. Moreover, he will be a happy man, even if his back is bent, his face lined, his life shattered. The eternal destiny of the world, the movement of life towards God has been realized in him; the hope of creation has found eternal reality in him: heaven.

SIGNS OF PROMISE

Signs of Promise

SOMETHING new is afoot in Christianity. Transforming forces are perceptible, deeply flowing currents which show that our faith is in a position to speak to the mankind of tomorrow. John XXIII called urgently in his opening address to the Council: "A step forward must be taken in establishing the truth and forming the conscience. This step will hold faithfully to the doctrine handed down but will also study and expound it in accordance with the modes of expression of modern thought." To many this demand may be unwelcome or even surprising. The Christian, however, will not take a decision simply because it suits him, or because he finds it pleasant, but because in the course of history he hears as it were the footsteps of the Lord whom he has to follow unconditionally. Is our faith capable of integrating the new sense of life which is emerging today? Can it offer the new humanity a spiritual home? We shall indicate a few characteristics of the Christian of tomorrow, without any attempt at completeness and even less at systematic treatment.

The Duty of Being Intelligent

The intellectual and social crises of the age have deeply influenced Catholic thinkers. The theologian has once more become an inquirer. He has to struggle with new problems and thus realizes that the deposit of revelation has in certain respects to be adapted. This intellectual attitude did not spring from an itch for novelty and innovation. We have been practically compelled by others to seek new answers to new questions. Craving for modernity played little or no part. Only stupid people will think that God prefers the stupid. Mental dullness, lack of understanding for partners in discussion, lack of general culture, are not signs of catholicity in anyone. It is not the duty of a Christian, for example, to find excuses for the faults of other Christians. Nor should he develop at all the sort of dangerous adroitness which produces a bland answer to any question or objection practically on the spot without reflection. Real believers know very well how difficult the ultimate questions of existence are. Why this urge to explain away and excuse everything? As Pope Leo XIII said, "God does not need our lies!" The virtue of intelligence consists in honesty of thought, openness to all truth, determined search for what is right. "Because you have rejected knowledge, I reject you . . . ," God said in the Book of Hosea the prophet. This still applies today. The fact that intellectual honesty and mental precision are found with increasing frequency among Christians today may be regarded as one of the most hopeful signs for the future of our Church.

Purify Our Idea of God

Another hopeful sign is that people no longer speak about God with quite such easy familiarity. They make no claim to know his mysteries and to guess his reactions. God's overwhelming difference is realized. This is surely a grace of our age. Something fundamentally important is taking place in this respect— God's growth in the mind of humanity. Instinctively people nowadays are turning away from the numerous caricatures of God, for example from the picture of the great policeman who is only interested in lawbreaking, the picture of a cosmic accountant registering our doings with terrifying precision, the picture of a powerful magician playing tricks with the logic of the world, the picture of a stop-gap who can continually be dragged in to explain cosmic phenomena, the picture of a torturer who seems intent on nothing but sending unbaptized infants and poor black men to hell. If we have reason to be grateful to atheists for anything at all at the present day, it is for preventing us cheating with our idea of God. We need have no fear of any changes in conceptions of man and the world. The greater man and the world become, the more God too will grow for us.

Humility of Mind

A critical mind, constantly measuring itself against reality, and therefore in the last resort a humble mind, is probably one of the best characteristics of modern man. This too corresponds to a Christian attitude of mind. Bergson had already pertinently observed that realism is one of the outstanding marks of the Christian. Faith remains, formulations pass. Faith frees us from the temptation of attributing to human values, persons and systems what belongs to the Absolute alone. It is a good thing that these ideas have become commonplaces in Catholicism. The very open discussions at the Council are a vivid example. People have stopped waiting for recognition and compliments. The Church is no longer triumphant. It knows that a Christian is not likely to have much success, at all events not enough to give himself airs about it. It is quite a big step if he can manage even for a moment to bring the eternal promise of the good news to the attention of his fellow men, considering the tremendous opacity of our world. Nowadays we need more witnesses, more lived Christianity and less propaganda. To quote Karl Rahner, it is not a Christian attitude to run "scandalized and criticizing behind the car that is carrying humanity into a new future." Negative testimony is nugatory. The positive, constructive and fundamental energies of Christianity must be released. This is what happened at the Council on an unexpected scale.

A Sanctity Concerned with the World

It seems to me that a new kind of saint is going to emerge at the present time. Of course such suppositions cannot be proved, they can only be sensed from the general mental atmosphere. The new kind of saint will, I imagine, be a human being who is seriously concerned for right action on the created level, who is very sensitive to the moment of grace, sinks into the world as it were in order to transform it. Every domain of the world will imply a Christian duty for him. He will be capable of moving from the splendid realm of abstract principles into the hurly-burly of historically appropriate prescriptions. He will know that a Christian style of things is unemphatic, indirect and serviceable. In quiet, unobtrusive people, by way of suffering sometimes, the world is being recovered as God's possession. The real future of the Church rests with them.

The Personal Way

There is a good deal of talk now about a changeover to a "Christianity of personal decision." In a world where religions, Churches, denominations and ideologies stand side by side with equal rights, and the individual no longer has the security of a well-marked religious domain, people often have to struggle through lengthy crises towards a personal decision of faith. The fact that many Catholics nowadays feel they must find their own personal way to God is both significant and promises well for the future. We have rediscovered individual spiritual gifts once more. It is astonishing how freely and clearly insights of this sort are expressed now in the Catholic Church, and how quickly the laity grasp them. Even only a few years ago things were very different. The present-day Catholic seems to have a greater understanding of what his individual search for God (described quite simply as the imitation of Christ) involves, and its importance for the whole of Christendom. It is also remarkable how often now one meets Catholics (though of course they are relatively few, for considerations of this kind are always a matter of an *élite*) who scrutinize closely their motives for choosing a profession, who won't allow themselves to be pushed into a position in life by mere impulse, or even by motives permissible in themselves, such as favourable working conditions, high salary, prospects of advancement. They ask themselves whether their profession will make it possible for them to bear that personal witness to Christ to which as Christians they are called. There are people today who reject a profession on grounds of this kind. As far as they are concerned it is out of the question, whatever wealth, well-being and influence it may promise.

✓ *Christocentric Piety*

It is a great joy to see how the younger generation is impressed by the personality of Christ. It is true that they do not see him in the way that has been familiar for centuries, as the blessed Redeemer. They don't like pretty-pretty ways of presenting this incomparably and immeasurably rich, inexhaustibly deep personality, and have no use for any kind of talk that is phoney, odd or dishonest. People have an acute sense of what is genuine, spontaneous and honest. Consequently they respond to the most genuine, spontaneous and honest person who ever existed in our world. A great change is taking place in Catholic piety. For example, the tremendous vision of Christ in the Revelation to John is psychologically much closer to us than the picture of Christ of our fathers' time. Many Catholics wonder now how they are to pray at all to this tremendous Christ. They are embarrassed, almost ashamed in their prayer, which is, in fact, a sign that something genuine and of profoundly human significance is taking place.

✓ *A Demanding Religion*

As Vatican II impressively explained, the Christian can never in any branch of personal life and faith act as if he were simply in calm possession. He is engaged in a search. This is a sign of vitality. By becoming more personal, Christianity loses nothing of its gravity and its rigour. The future belongs to those who set their hearts on what is humanly unattainable. Faith of that kind can only be found in personal devotion to Christ, and only such personal dedication makes a man a real Christian. It is the way the Christian becomes a visible expression of God in the world. We are pointers to Christ. That is what our Christian life demands of us.

Decline of Clericalism

The decline of clericalism is important for the future of Catholicism; it is not merely factual decline, but involves a change of mentality. There is a decline of external clericalism, by the lessening of the excessive influence of the Church on political life, as far as this involves an abuse of religion. There is also a decline of clericalism inside the Church through the freeing of the laity from clerical tutelage. The more decidedly the Catholic Church affirms its supernatural position, the more successfully it puts itself at the service of God's cause. Catholics feel this very strongly today, although we must honestly admit that many clerics still find it difficult to live up to the principle.

Positive Attitude to Christian Fraternity

There is a new understanding of fraternal service. Christians realize nowadays that someone who has never in his life given food to the hungry, drink to the thirsty, shelter to a stranger, who has never clothed the naked, comforted those in prison, is not a real Christian. He has missed the essence of Christianity.

It is astonishing how responsive Christians are now if one speaks to them in lectures, debates or private conversation about the future of humanity depending on a spirit of fraternity. Sympathy for the neighbour (leaving aside the question whether this is already genuine love for Christ) is welling up in the Christian soul with unsuspected force. It is a promising sign. It is not the only one. In this talk we have simply mentioned those that seemed important to us and which indicate an inner transformation. Externals always spring from some frame of mind. God grant that this diagnosis is correct. The chances could be missed.

CREATION AND
EVOLUTION

Creation and Evolution

ONE of the most important events of the present time is, as Pascual Jordan put it, that "science has ceased to be a source of irreligion." Today science and faith are no longer hostile. It is a vital duty for Christianity in the twentieth century to ensure that this discussion continues and is carried on openly and frankly.

John XXIII's shattering opening address to the Second Vatican Council affirmed in principle this openminded attitude of twentieth-century Christians:

In the daily exercise of our pastoral office, we sometimes have to listen, much to our regret, to voices of persons who, though burning with zeal, are not endowed with too much sense of discretion or measure. In these modern times they can see nothing but prevarication and ruin. They say that our era, in comparison with past eras, is getting worse, and they behave as though they had learned nothing from history, which is, none the less, the teacher of life. . . . We feel we must disagree with those prophets of gloom, who are always forecasting disaster. . . . In the present order of things, divine Providence is leading us to a new order of human relations which, by men's own efforts and even beyond their very expectations, are directed towards the fulfilment of God's superior and inscrutable designs.

What are then the characteristics of the "new men" who already regard themselves as the first representatives and heralds of man as he is going to be? They are marked by science, evolution and technology. What then is the attitude of Christianity to science, evolution and technology?

Science and Faith

The scientific spirit is acquired nowadays almost unconsciously, even by those without scientific training. This is the first element in the new attitude to the world. What is Christianity's judgment on the natural sciences?

The first, most general and all-decisive principle of the Christian attitude to science is that truth, every truth, is of divine origin. It is therefore impossible in principle for faith and science to contradict one another. There cannot be any real conflict between them, at most an apparent conflict. This of course does not in any way exclude the possibility that tensions may develop between faith and science and that these may only be solved by slow, tedious and, on occasion, tragic efforts. But to the extent that science discovers truth, it cannot stand in contradiction to Christian faith.

This seems to us to be the only correct Christian attitude to the sciences, which are now disclosing to man a universe of breathtaking dimensions. We regard this very fact as full of promise, and the greater the world becomes and the more powerful the human mind, the greater we can also conceive God to be.

Evolution

The most significant transformation of our world-view at present taking place is in the domain of evolutionary theory. Since the Renaissance, a change has taken place in the mind of humanity. A static has been replaced by a dynamic world-view. In a first phase (Galileo), mankind discovered that the earth moves and is not the sole and motionless centre of the universe. In a second phase (Darwin), mankind realized that cosmic movement and change has also to be extended to all terrestrial life. In a third phase (today), we are beginning to realize that the process of hominization is not yet closed by any means. The same movement which out of the matter of the universe formed a cosmos, an ordered world, and continued its course in the ascent of life, continues to live in us and is driving human history towards what transcends humanity. The evolution of the universe comes to completion in man, but he still stands at the beginning of his full humanization. A Christianity which shut itself off now from this development, even momentarily (as happened in the case of Galileo and later in that of Darwin), would lose its vitality and attraction. What then is the attitude of the Catholic Church to the doctrine of evolution?

Evolution is accepted as an indubitable fact by the modern scientist. He considers the general theory of evolution, which includes that of mankind, to be a fundamental and scientifically established conception. The question no longer arises for him whether evolution has taken place, but only how it took place, what the mechanisms of evolution are. The official magisterium of the Church has expressly recognized this position held by scientists, and has confirmed that it is not in contradiction with the teaching of revelation.

Three documents are of prime importance in this connection. First Pius XII's address to the Papal Academy of Sciences in 1941; secondly the Letter of the Secretary of the Biblical Commission in 1943; thirdly the Encyclical *Humani Generis* in 1950. Earlier Church pronouncements on the question have to be interpreted in the sense of these three documents.

For our purpose, four points are of particular importance in the teaching of these three documents. In the first place the doctrine of evolution is officially permitted and may be made the subject of serious and careful discussion. This implies that it does not contradict revelation. *Humani Generis* says in so many words, ". . . the Church's magisterium does not forbid the doctrine of evolution . . . in the present state of the sciences and of theology . . . being made the object of research and specialist discussion." Secondly, the human mind or soul is not a product of evolution. The official permission does not apply to the kind of evolutionary theory which suppresses the specific difference between spirit and matter. The human soul, both at the beginning of hominization and in each individual human being, is created directly by God. It is not said how this direct creation is to be envisaged. The provisional guideline in *Humani Generis* says that discussion among specialists should be restricted to the origin of the human body and its evolution from lower organic forms. Thirdly, it is stressed that the Christian may not act "as if the origin of the human body from already existing living matter were already a certain truth absolutely demonstrated by the evidence discovered so far and the inferences drawn from it."

Two things must be taken into consideration here.

The encyclical was written in 1950 and refers to the scientific situation as it was at that time. Furthermore, the Church's magisterium appears to be attempting to impose on the Catholic scientist a judgment regarding the degree of certainty of his secular knowledge. This raises the delicate question whether the magisterium is competent to estimate the certainty achieved by secular science. In our opinion, and in accordance with the principles of theology, the answer to this must quite unambiguously be No. Fourthly, a warning is given against polygenism. As opposed to monogenism (which teaches the biological origin of the whole of present-day humanity from one human pair), polygenism assumes that present-day humanity owes its origin to a number of progenitors. "Present-day humanity" in this connection means the *homo sapiens* group. It is therefore not a question of the other stages of human evolution, for example, Neanderthal man, Pithecanthropus, Australopithecus. This means that monogenism does not necessarily exclude "successive polygenism." The magisterium's warning refers simply and solely to the polygenetic mode of descent of the *homo sapiens* group. Contemporary anthropological research, however, is clearly tending in the direction of polygenism, in the sense of polygenetic descent of the *homo sapiens* group. It is certainly not doing so out of a spirit of contradiction, but for reasons which merit attention. On the other hand it generally holds fast to the so-called "monophyletic" origin of mankind. In other words it assumes that the leap of hominization occurred within a genetically homogeneous animal group, that is, that mankind does not descend from several specifically distinct ancestors. In short, present-day anthropology appears to favour the specific unity of mankind and its origin from a single species, but is inclined to regard the leap of hominization as occurring not at one point but in numerous individuals.

Why did the Church issue a warning against polygenism? Because at that time a polygenetic perspective seemed to the Church to threaten the unity of the history of salvation and above all the doctrine of original sin. The following should, however, be noted in this connection. The encyclical does not assert the incompatibility of polygenism with Catholic teaching on original sin, but merely says its compatibility is not evident: *"cum nequaquam appareat quomodo:* it is not at all clear how . . ." (one of the most brilliantly non-committal turns of phrase of the magisterium). It is not said that such insight may come later, but neither does it say that it is excluded for all time.

If we now try to draw up an interim statement, it is plain that these Church pronouncements, taken as a whole, create a very positive and friendly atmosphere between theologians and natural scientists in the question of evolution. If such is the case, however, one might wonder why the Church opposed the idea of evolution for so long. On this it must be noted that the Catholic Church as such never did officially oppose the idea of evolution, except in one document, a declaration of the Cologne diocesan synod in 1860, but this is disregarded now by everyone, as having no dogmatic authority. It has always been permissible, not merely since Pius XII, for a Catholic to be an evolutionist. Some of the greatest Fathers of the Church (Irenaeus of Lyons, Gregory of Nyssa and Augustine) in fact held a theory of evolution. Not of course in the present-day sense. They knew nothing of gene mutation and chromosome changes. But their fundamental insight involved an evolutionary conception. Augustine's view, for example, was very modern, and his full intuition has only very recently been recognized. For him, creation at the beginning of time meant that in the beginning God brought into existence a concentration of all energies and powers in which everything was seminally contained. He then caused these energies to act according to their inherent laws. A reality pregnant with the future was created at the beginning of time, still formless, but already containing all forms of being within itself.

The case was different, of course, as regards individual Catholics (and Protestants, for there was no difference in their judgment on evolution), which in practice means most Catholic theologians and philosophers from the middle of the last century until the first decades of the present century. Only then was there a shift of opinion in theological circles. Their hostile attitude towards the theory of evolution was chiefly due to a fundamental lack of clarity.

They took their stand on the principle that the testimony of holy Scripture is to be understood "literally." At the same time they tacitly assumed that the Bible is intended to convey scientific information. But that is exactly what is not so. The Bible is not a scientific text-book, it is a message of salvation. God spoke to men so that real people could understand him, which means he used the world of images and ideas of men who lived thousands of years ago in the East. In a biblical account we have therefore to distinguish between the message of salvation and the form of the message, between statement and mode of expression, between what is said and how it is said. If we do not do so, we are not taking the biblical account more "literally," we are simply misunderstanding it. Consequently we must first determine what literary genre a biblical account belongs to, if we are to distinguish precisely its content from its form.

If these fundamental insights (formulated in greater

detail in Karl Rahner's works) are applied to the two creation accounts in Genesis, we may conclude, to put it briefly, that they are not eye-witness accounts, documentaries on the events of creation at the beginning of time. They are statements about the fact of creation. If this principle is correct, everything that the authors could know about the beginning of things by reflection on their own situation belongs to the content of statement, while what they could not know by such reflection must be regarded as part of the form of expression.

Let us now see how this principle applies to the Genesis account of the special creation of man. Genesis states that God took dust from the ground, formed man of it, just as potters make different utensils out of clay, then took this form and breathed the breath of life into its nostrils, "and man became a living being." A threefold statement can be discerned in this image. In the first place, man is not created by God out of nothing; man is materially dependent on the world. It is not said what kind of material dependence is expressed by the image of the dust of the earth. The matter might just as well have been an already existing highly-developed animal form. The theological point here is the fundamentally terrestrial, earthbound nature of man, his involvement in the world. Secondly, although man is so essentially a part of the earth, he is nevertheless radically different from all other creatures. God creates him as it were with his own hands to be his partner. A direct relation is affirmed of man to God, although man has to live and achieve this relation to God in a situation which binds him to the earth. Thirdly, this direct relation to God, which distinguishes man from all other creatures, springs from the fact that man bears within him the breath of God, that is to say, he is spiritual, and so transcends the world and the animals. Earthly nature, direct relation to God, spirituality, these seem to be what is contained and affirmed in this account of creation. All the rest is mode of statement, representative schema, garb, concrete embodiment of the content with the help of imagery drawn from a particular civilization. And these three essential elements can be known by a religious man in any situation of life.

In a similar way the other accounts of origins (creation of the world, the work of the six days, formation of woman from Adam's rib, original paradisal state, the way original sin occurred) could be disengaged from their literary form and mode of representation and reduced to their essential affirmations. But this would lead us too far. One thing should, however, have already become clear. The account of creation, understood in this way, does not contradict in any way the scientific bases of the theory of evolution, quite the contrary.

The synthesis of evolutionary theory and Christian faith outlined by Teilhard de Chardin is in harmony with this fact.

Creation and evolution are not contradictory for Teilhard de Chardin. The concrete structure of evolution is, in fact, the side of God's creative activity which is visible to man. That creative activity is not a violent insertion of things into an already completed world, but an emergence and production of forms from the womb of reality until man is reached, and even beyond. For Teilhard, the cosmos was a process of development maturing stage by stage over thousands of millions of years towards its fulfilment, feeling its way forwards through increasing complexity and interiorization of matter. In this process, man stands in the direct line of the total tendency of life.

Teilhard emphasizes that man is no longer, as it was

possible to think in former times, the changeless centre of an already completed world. Instead, as far as we can judge, he is the spear-point of cosmic evolution which is moving towards even greater spiritual interiorization. Man is evolution which has become conscious of itself, says Teilhard, quoting Julian Huxley with approval. Man bears the destiny of the universe. The cosmic will to life flows through him. But man himself is not yet complete. He is an evolving being. The process of hominization is not yet complete. Man is only at the beginning of his self-development, with a future which must be respected, not squandered. Fidelity to genuine humanity, therefore, means fidelity not only to the past and the present, but also to the future. And in this respect the intensified evolutionary pressure on humanity deserves particular notice. What future is humanity being impelled towards? Teilhard's answer is, that humanity is being impelled in the direction of a general convergence of all energies.

The universe as a single evolutionary development tends increasingly to converge, and is therefore conical in form. In man, the evolutionary process finally narrows, and with the breakthrough into the spiritual, evolution has concentrated for ever in man. In the light of a systematic and coherent theory of evolution, the present age appears to be a turning-point in the history of humanity. Individuals are beginning to come together; a closer network of spiritual links is being woven between them. Groups, units, nations and families of nations are beginning to become more transparent to one another, more receptive, more open, more capable of association. What is in question, according to Teilhard, is a planetary "involution," an all-inclusive convergence of mankind. The inalienable values of the person must not be jeopardized by this. It must not suppress the highest achievement of cosmic evolution, which is the human person, or lead to totalitarianism. On the other hand, a purely juridical and political unification of mankind is incapable of ever satisfying the profound desire for organic unity which has awakened in the human soul.

The final convergence of the universe, which is to be achieved in humanity, cannot take place in humanity alone. For Teilhard de Chardin, only one possibility remains open. Humanity must become one through what transcends mankind, which at the same time is a personal being and is therefore able to safeguard the personal uniqueness of every human being while at the same time uniting all human beings within itself—in other words, God. This is the point, Teilhard says, at which the problem of God is raised for science by evolution, for the only way evolution can continue its course is with God as its focus and head.

This does not yet express, however, the ultimate and essential feature of Teilhard de Chardin's interpretation of the world. The evolution of the universe does not converge simply on a transcendent God, but on the God-man. If mankind is to achieve the last evolutionary leap, that of union with God, the abyss of absolute transcendence between God and man must be overcome. There must be someone who is both man and God and whose scope is such that he can assume into himself, into his body, the whole of humanity. A God-man is, therefore, the focus, the omega-point of evolution. He lives in the risen state, that is, of all-pervading, pneumatic power, a transfigured God-man, who builds up the plenitude of his reality out of unified humanity. To sum up this worldview in a few sentences, we cannot do better than refer to the introductory lines of a short work of Teilhard de Chardin, *Comment je crois.* "I believe that the universe is an evolutionary process. I believe that evolution tends in the direction of spirit. I believe that spirit culminates in the personal. I believe that the consummation of the personal is the cosmic Christ."

Perhaps the most important thing in all this is that Teilhard de Chardin presents the example of a man who was able once more to see and experience the world with religious emotion, who discerned a new presence of God in the world, in fact the only presence of God which is given to men, the presence of God in Jesus Christ. What Teilhard has done is irrevocable. It has set up in Christian thought a powerful tendency towards a Christocentric view of the cosmos. Even if certain ideas of Teilhard eventually prove to be imprecise, obsolete or even faulty, this fundamental tendency will leave its mark on future generations of Christians, on the "new man." The transformation of our world-view which Teilhard de Chardin heralds will have deep and far-reaching consequences. It affects man as a whole in his understanding of himself and the world, and even in his relation to him whom man calls God.

Technology

The new type of human being more and more takes his decisive stamp from the natural sciences. The attitude to life of the scientist influences the whole population now. The man of the future will stand in a completely new relation to technology. He will be dominated by the scientific spirit, which he will build into a style of life. His psychological pattern will be determined chiefly by his technical function. What will be the chief characteristics of a humanity thus

stamped by technology and science? Men will transform the world, in fact they will give it its complete
form for the first time.

The first characteristic of this new type of man is
his purposefulness. He sees himself constantly faced
with tasks to fulfil. His mental attitude is essentially
purposive. His mind is dominated by objective considerations. This entails a series of other characteristics, tenacity, perseverance, concentration, conscien-
tiousness and self-discipline. He lives in a world
which is planned through and through. The order of
his procedures is dictated by the laws and nature of
his technical material, and is therefore imposed on
him in all essentials by the work he is doing.

A second trait is bound up with this. The new type
of man is "professional," strictly objective. His whole
attention has to be guided by the demands of the
work itself. The object itself forms him. And he can
only enter into contact with the object with extreme
concentration and by excluding subjective influences.
His fundamental attitude is one of attending to the
truth of things themselves, a kind of earthly piety. No
approximation is possible. Only hard facts count.

This attitude reveals another feature of the new
kind of man who is emerging, his dedication. He has
to abandon his subjectivity, put himself in parenthe-
ses, so to speak. Everything about him is geared to
efficiency; finishing the job is what matters. In
technological and scientific activity there can be no
indulgence, no personal concessions, no shirking.
Knowledge must really stem from the object. Such
an attitude detaches a man from caprice and wilful-
ness.

A fourth trait follows from all this, sobriety. This
kind of human being is more critical, mistrustful and
even sceptical than previous generations. He will not

let himself in for anything risky. What has been laboriously achieved and built up must not be jeopardized. This human type knows that by his ability, discipline and professional precision he gives human society new solidity. In other domains of social organization he has the impression there is nothing but conflict, divergent opinions, vagueness and chatter, in the human sciences, in politics, philosophy and religion. His attitude to society is unemotional, he has no patent schemes or rhetoric. In his view the real formative social forces are sober clarity, an eye for the essential, objectivity, strict self-discipline. Only characteristics of this kind are capable, in his view, of building the world of the future and of saving the present age from the chaos which threatens it. It was men with this kind of attitude who came to the fore in the Kennedy administration, for example, as the president's staff of personal advisers.

A fifth trait accompanies sobriety of this kind, which as an ethical attitude is based on very severe self-discipline. The technologist takes it for granted that he has to fit into a plan of work. The work itself, the very meaning of the activity, demands an enormous amount of adaptation and system. Nevertheless this attitude is not one of subordination and does not really consist in receiving orders. In a technically well-organized concern it is not possible just to give out orders. In the strict sense there are no subordinates. Everyone is directed by an objective discipline inherent in the nature of the technical problem, and all are equal in dignity. The more complicated a technical problem is, the more the individual technologists must collaborate in team work. Each has to work with the utmost precision in his own field, but the project can only be achieved by the collaboration of all.

Consequently solidarity may be regarded as the

sixth characteristic of the new type of man. The ability
to work together in groups and teams is increasingly a
fundamental qualification in the technological profes-
sions. Already a very significant sociological selection
is taking place in this respect. The era of great per-
sonalities, of men of lonely greatness, seems to be over.
The work and goal are what count, not personal
idiosyncrasies and judgments. Objective agreement,
unemotional comradeship, self-effacement in view of
the common task, dedication and tolerance are the
attitudes which emerge in this new feeling for solidarity. This kind of working solidarity already links the
whole earth. A man with a technological and scientific formation is already closer to a technologist from
another nation or race than to his neighbour who has
been educated in the humanities. A clearly recognizable affinity is constantly bringing together these new
men of a new age, and this attraction seems to know
no impenetrable frontiers, no social, racial or religious
bounds.

This indicates the seventh characteristic of this new
type of man. His outlook is world-wide, universal in
range, not only in the sense that he is aware and
thinks in terms of the whole earth, but also in the
sense that he feels a kinship with the whole cosmos.
Technological man does not regard any realm of the
universe as closed to him in principle, whether it is a
question of the stellar abysses of the universe, the
subatomic structure of matter or the bio-physical
structure of man. He is now busy starting to apply his
power of technical manipulation to man himself, in
other words to make himself the object of planning.
The most recent experiments in human biological
planning are artificial insemination, positive and negative eugenics, determination of sex in the embryo,
artificial breeding of human beings outside the

womb, parthogenesis, research into twins, storage of organs and tissues for transplantation, artificial increase of brain cells, immunization, lengthening the life-span. These technologists consider that the most urgent problem today is to prevent the decline in quality of the genetic stock by the selective methods of systematic breeding; the maintenance of health and further human development in the future can only be ensured by raising the genetic level.

The results of experimental biology are already making it feasible to alter man's physical and psychological constitution considerably. There are even more possibilities, which cannot be realized at present, it is true, but which are not definitely excluded for the future. The attention of Christians needs to be drawn to the benefits and dangers of this development. There are some grounds for hope, but many reasons for fear. The new man regards the whole world and himself as raw material from which he intends to create a new world and a new humanity on a pattern designed by himself.

The immensity of the cosmos has opened out before him. He is listening to the hidden greatness to which he has devoted himself. His taciturnity is therefore an expression of his concentrated strength. Everything petty and trivial seems embarrassing and profoundly alien to him. How could a man of this kind endure for long the *petit bourgeois,* paltry and undignified God so often presented to him?

From the overwhelming experience of the tremendous task ahead, the new men draw profound confidence, which dominates their whole mentality. This is the ninth and final trait in our description of technological man. He is the servant of the future, the shaper of a new earth. He is inspired by an ethos of service. Technological work demands matter-of-fact unselfishness. The technologist knows that he is not working for himself, that once finished, a project will serve other people. This ethos makes him confident that what he creates is really of service.

To many people, the future may appear threatening, but the new man of the technological era feels sure he will master it somehow or another, in the same way that he masters any other technical problem. By careful observance of the laws of nature and by precision of technical performance, he is certain of success. A new kind of serenity is emerging in this way, and giving rise to a new attitude to the world, the steady calm and cool imperturbability of a man who has the most dangerous powers of nature at hand but knows that he can control them. All this involves a conviction that the world is good, and that as long as we attend to the underlying patterns which regulate this world, confidence is well-founded. This is perhaps the point at which this kind of man advances furthest into the domain of metaphysics and religion.

This necessarily incomplete description of the newly emerging attitude to the world has in no sense been concerned to describe an ideal type. Some features of this kind of human being appear alien to us, in fact human nature seems in some ways impoverished in him. At the same time, however, the Christian of today must see in the emergence of the technological mind a grace intended by God for this moment of the world's history. And a grace always involves a task to be fulfilled.

The goal of existence for the new type of man seems to consist in changing and transforming the world, in fact in giving it for the first time its really complete form. Everywhere he finds that the world is imperfect but perfectible. He wants to master the cosmos and make a home and country for us inside a threatened world, to open up the world, subject it to man, create a universe which will permit man to be a new man, to transform the world into a place where it is possible to live a human life. Now this is not merely a human task, it is in fact in accordance with God's intentions.

In his letter to the Christians in Philippi, Paul describes the Christians' expectation as follows: "We await . . . the Lord Jesus Christ, who will change our lowly body to be like his glorious body, by the power which enables him even to subject all things to himself." At the end of the Revelation to John, Christ says, "I make all things new." At the end of the history of salvation, therefore, there is a completely transfigured world, Christ's *pleroma*: Christ, built up out of human beings and surrounded by a transfigured world. The Fathers of the Church were never tired of speaking of the change, transformation, metamorphosis and renewal of our world. What is the relation between this eschatological transformation of the world into heaven, into an essential domain of direct contact with God, and our present universe, which men are working to reshape?

Creation and transformation form one single whole for God. The world definitively created is the world transformed into glory. Our works are not rejected by the Christ who makes all things new, they are made radiant and raised to the plane of finality. The new man can therefore feel himself close to Christ. He is God's instrument in the great work of transforming the world. To realize this, to catch some glimpse of the divine, eschatological dimensions of our earthly activities, is the grace bestowed on our age.